The History and Religion
of Israel

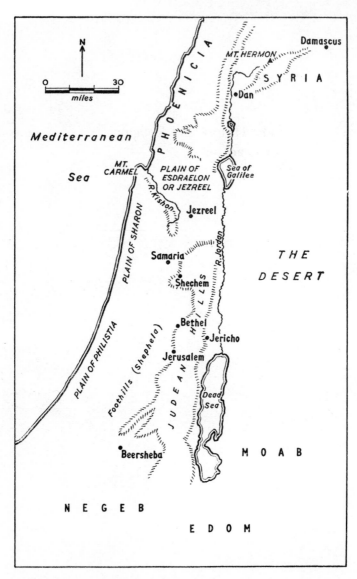

A physical map of Palestine

The History and Religion of Israel

from the death of Solomon to the fall of Jerusalem

LEVI DAWSON BD PhD

 Evans Brothers Limited

Published by Evans Brothers Limited
Montague House Russell Square London WC1B 5BX
Evans Brothers (Nigeria) Limited
© LEVI DAWSON 1968
First Published 1968
Reprinted 1974, 1975, 1976, 1977, 1979

Printed in Great Britain by
T. & A. Constable Ltd.
Hopetoun Street, Edinburgh
ISBN 0 237 28006 X   PRA 6255

Preface

This book has been written to help students to understand an important period of Biblical history. The needs of those preparing for G.C.E. O-Level Examinations have been especially kept in mind, but it is hoped that those preparing for A-Level will find it of use, as well as those Church groups seeking a closer acquaintance with the Bible.

Students are reminded that no textbook can take the place of accurate study of the Biblical text. This book is intended to help the reader to understand that text. Each chapter is based upon certain passages from the Old Testament and these must be read and studied. There is no substitute for this.

Quotations are from the *Revised Standard Version* but the references apply of course to any other version used.

A Glossary of explanatory notes has been added together with questions which can serve as exercises. The author gratefully acknowledges the permission of the University of London to include questions which have been set at G.C.E. O-Level Examinations of that University.

L. D.

Tiffin Girls' School
Kingston-upon-Thames
March 1968

Contents

Preface 5

1 Setting the Scene 9
2 Reading the History 12
3 The Division of the Kingdom 18
4 Jeroboam and his Successors 23
5 Rehoboam and his Successors 27
6 Omri and Ahab 31
7 Israel and Judah after Ahab 42
8 Revolution 50
9 The Dynasty of Jehu 56
10 Amos 62
11 The Fall of Israel 67
12 Hosea 72
13 The Decline of Judah 77
14 The Prophet Isaiah 83
15 The Reign of Hezekiah 90
16 Micah 97
17 The Contribution of the Eighth-Century 101
    Prophets
18 Manasseh 106
19 Josiah 109
20 The Book of Deuteronomy 114
21 The Fall of Judah 119
22 Jeremiah 125
23 The Message of Jeremiah 131

Note on the Books of *Kings* and *Chronicles* 139

Glossary 143

CHARTS

The Chart to the fall of Samaria   82
Kings of Judah after the fall of Samaria   124
The Kings of Assyria   140
The Kings of Syria   141

MAPS AND DIAGRAMS

A physical map of Palestine   *frontispiece*
The lands between the Nile and the Persian Gulf   11
The Kingdoms of Israel and Judah   22
Places visited by Elijah   37
Places visited by Elisha   48
Palestine during the time of the Syrian conquest,
      850-800 BC   55
Palestine in the time of Jeroboam II   61
The victory of Assyria   69
Palestine after the fall of Samaria, 722 BC   76
The Syro-Ephraimite War   79
The Empire of Assyria, *c.* 700 BC   91
The clash of empires   120

Acknowledgement

Cover photograph, "Ushering in the Holy Days with Shofar, the ram's horn," by kind permission of the Israel Government Tourist Board.

CHAPTER 1

Setting the Scene

During the period of history we are to study we shall be watching a great drama played before our eyes. The first thing then is to make sure of the setting. We must see the scenery against which the play is to unfold.

This drama is played on a very small stage. Palestine itself is a very small country – about one-fifth of the size of Scotland, half the size of Belgium and one-third the size of Switzerland. From Dan to Beersheba (which was the Hebrew way of saying 'from Land's End to John o' Groats') the distance is only 150 miles. The distance across Palestine from the Mediterranean to the Jordan is at its widest part only 50 miles. Yet within this small area are great extremes. To go from Jerusalem to Jericho one would have to descend 3,000 feet in 15 miles, and go in that descent from the sharp mountain air of the capital city to a city of palms with a tropical climate. The mountains of the north (Hermon is 9,000 feet and Lebanon 6,000 feet) are always capped with snow. The Dead Sea in the south (1,275 feet below sea-level and as deep again) is surrounded by thick mists and stifling heat.

During the summer, that is from May to October, the sun beats down mercilessly, scorching everything. The winter months from December to February are times of heavy rain and extreme cold. The early rains of October and November break the drought and soften the land, whilst the 'latter rains' of March and April give the crops the last watering before the drought starts again.

9

Now take a look at a map (*frontispiece*). The really important map shows the hills and rivers because these are the things that determine the life of man. If you stood on the heights of Jerusalem and looked north you would see stretching before you a range of limestone hills as far as the Kishon valley (known as the Plain of Esdraelon or Jezreel) and then rising again to the hills of Galilee in the north. To the south the hills would get broader until at last they disappeared into the Negeb (south) which is sheer desert.

Between this range of hills and the sea is a coastal plain except where it is cut by the spur of hills which ends in Carmel. Between the plain and the hill country in the south is a range of foothills known as the Shephelah.

All the chief events of Hebrew history for a thousand years take place between the Kishon Valley and the Negeb. The real history is played out on a stage much smaller than Palestine itself. The Hebrew was a man of the highlands and of that part of highland country between Esdraelon and the desert.

Behind this small stage, however, there is a much wider background. Look now at another map (on p. 11), a map that shows the area from the Nile to the two rivers of Mesopotamia, the Euphrates and the Tigris. If you wanted to go from Egypt to Babylon, which way would you go? The distance as the crow flies would seem the obvious way to travel. But that way is through a great desert which would be very difficult to cross. The normal way would be by travelling up the coastal plain, through Esdraelon to Galilee, and then by a route rather like a crescent to the upper valley of the Euphrates. This route passed through what was called the 'Fertile Crescent'* because the area was fertile compared with the desert around.

During the time of our story, Egypt and Mesopotamia were the two great centres of empire, civilisation and wealth. They were the two most thickly populated areas of the Bible world. It is easy to see, therefore, that traders and

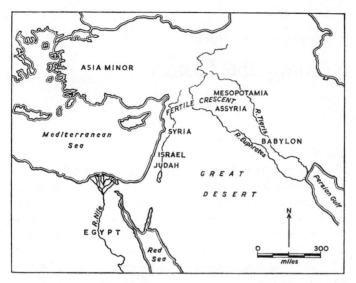

The lands between the Nile and the Persian Gulf

others who wanted to pass from one to the other would have to go through Palestine. When the time came, as come it did, for one country to attack another, the armies had to march through Palestine. Palestine occupied, therefore, a situation similar to that occupied by Belgium in the two great European wars. Although a neutral state she was a natural 'buffer' between the two empires and however much she wanted to do so, she could not keep apart from world affairs.

This, then, is the stage setting. Make sure you know these two maps. Make sure you know where the hills and rivers are and as you study the history try to see it all the time against the background of the stage on which it is played.

CHAPTER 2

Reading the History

The Point of View

Bible history is written from a particular point of view.
The writers assume that they are writing not so much
about the activity of men as about the activity of God. The
events of history are interpreted as God's planned activity,
planned with His own purpose in mind. The historian is
always conscious that the living God is working in history
and this God meets with men in the experiences of everyday life.

As you know, the Bible consists of various documents put
together. The part that we are to study was gathered together by a man known as the Deuteronomic historian. In
621 BC a book was found in the Temple at Jerusalem which
caused a great religious revival in Israel. This so inspired
one man that on its basis he wrote the history of Israel in
Palestine, collecting and using earlier sources as he thought
best. This history is found in the books *Joshua* to *II Kings*.
The old book which was found in the Temple formed the
core of our present book of *Deuteronomy*. It consists of a
statement of the relation between the faith of Israel and
their occupation of the land of Palestine. God gave them
this 'promised land'. In the book of *Deuteronomy* they are
given the terms by which they are to be allowed to keep it.
Here is what God requires of His people if they are to remain in possession of the land.

Using this as his introduction, the Deuteronomic historian tells the story of the people in the promised land and

gives his interpretation of why the land was lost. The history, therefore, covers the period between the entry into Palestine following the Exodus from Egypt, and the deportation to Babylon in 586 BC.

The history is interpreted in the light of the writer's fundamental belief that God brings blessing to those who are obedient to Him and judgment upon those who disobey Him. This means that men must love God with heart and soul and strength, and obey Him in all things. The people are bound to God by the Covenant which was made at Sinai. Because the word 'Covenant'* sums up the Israelite's idea of his relationship to God we must see what it meant.

When Moses led the Israelites out of Egypt he brought them to Mount Sinai. While they were there Moses went up the Mountain and received a message from God. This was that God had chosen these people to be His own. He called them to join in a Covenant, i.e. to make an agreement with Him. They must promise to obey Him and He would promise to look after them and defend them. To us this seems very much like a bargain. That is because we are used to the idea of trade and exchanging goods for money. The Hebrew was not a trader and he did not think of the Covenant in that way. God, out of His mercy and love, had chosen Israel and in gratitude Israel must obey Him. That meant that no idols must be worshipped and the people must put their trust in God alone. The Covenant was sealed at Sinai with solemn promises and now Israel and God belonged to each other.

In order that the people may be loyal to this Covenant, the book of *Deuteronomy* demands that worship must be centralised in Jerusalem and that all outlying sanctuaries, which can so easily become places of idolatry, be closed. This explains the historian's criticism of all the kings who did not destroy the 'high places'*. A judgment is passed on all the kings. Only two, Hezekiah and Josiah, are unreservedly praised. Many are condemned completely and

13

others receive only grudging praise if they fail to remove the 'high places'.

The judgment of the historian is made, not in terms of a king's diplomacy and military power, but entirely in terms of whether he was faithful to God or not. This does not mean that the history is inaccurate. It does mean, however, that we must keep in mind all the time the point of view of the writer.

The Way of Writing

For the greater part of this period the history of Palestine is the history of two separate kingdoms existing side by side. The historian jumps from one to the other in what seems to be a most confusing way. The reason for this is quite clear. He has no standard calendar by which to date the various kings and he can only date one by reference to the other, that is, he can only date a king of Israel by saying what king of Judah was reigning at the time. Accordingly he tells the story of the reign of, shall we say, a king of Israel. When the king dies, the historian turns to Judah and discusses the kings who reigned during the reign of the king of Israel. When he comes to the last king of Judah in the period, he carries the story to the end of his reign and then reverts to Israel. This can be most confusing to us until we find a way to make it clear.

First of all, however, let us notice the method of writing. Each reign is dealt with according to a kind of formula, and this can be seen as a pattern under five sections.

1. The historian begins, 'In the "x" year of A, king of Israel, B, king of Judah, began to reign' or 'In the "y" year of the reign of C, king of Judah, D, king of Israel began to reign.'

2. Next, in the case of the kings of Israel, he gives the length of the reign and the place of the capital. In the case of the kings of Judah he gives the king's age, length of reign and the name of the queen mother.

3. In the case of the kings of Israel, he goes on to state that 'he did that which was evil in the sight of the Lord, and walked in the way of Jeroboam and his sin which made Israel to sin'.

In the case of the kings of Judah he estimates his worth in comparison with 'David his father'.

4. The reader is referred to the rest of his acts which he can read for himself in either 'The Book of the Chronicles of the Kings of Israel' or 'The Book of the Chronicles of the Kings of Judah'.

(*NB* This does not refer to our books of *Chronicles* in the Bible, but to books known to the writer which have since been lost.)

5. The statement that the king slept with his fathers and someone else reigned in his stead.

You can see examples of this if you look up the account of the reign of Jehoshaphat in *I Kings* 22 *41-50*. He was a king of Judah. An example of a king of Israel can be found in *I Kings* 15 *25-32*. There are, of course, many other examples.

How to get hold of the History
We must find a means by which we can understand our way in this seeming maze. We have to find a method by which we can see clearly the history of the two kingdoms side by side, and also take into account the relationships of these kingdoms with the surrounding nations. Look again at the map of the larger stage (p. 11) and put down the nations as you read them from west to east. You will get a list like this:

Egypt   Judah   Israel   Syria   Mesopotamia

Now make a number of columns headed by each one of these. These columns are to be filled in as we study the history so that we can see at a glance what is happening.

15

Here would be the chart for the first part of our period.

Time Chart

Important Kings in italics

Egypt	Judah	Israel	Syria	Mesopotamia
900 BC	*Rehoboam*	*Jeroboam I*		
Shishak ⟶				
	Abijah			
		Nadab		
	Asa ⟵——	Baasha ⟵——	*Benhadad I*	

N.B. The arrows indicate invasions.

A glance at this will remind you that certain kings were reigning in Israel and Judah at the time of certain other kings elsewhere. You will also see that during the reign of Rehoboam, Shishak invaded Palestine from Egypt. Also, when Asa was king of Judah he was attacked by Baasha, king of Israel. Asa appealed for help to Benhadad, king of Syria, who attacked Baasha and compelled him to withdraw from attacking Judah. We shall continue this chart as we continue our study. Make your own. It will not only help you to understand what is happening but will be of great value when you come to your revision.

One further word before we turn to watch the drama of this period. Above everything else read the passages in the Bible set for study. The chapters which follow are based upon the assumption that you will read the Bible passages. Remember that you will be examined not on any particular textbook or on your teacher's notes, but on the text of the Bible itself. If you read it with the help the book can give, you will find it a very thrilling story indeed.

As you read this book you will see some words are marked

with an asterisk, so *. This means that a note about them will be found in the Glossary at the end of the book.

NOTE ON THE NAME OF GOD

The Hebrew had a great sense of the majesty and holiness of God. His reverence for the Name of God was so great that he would never pronounce it. When he wrote it, he wrote it without the vowels so that it would not be pronounced. The consonants of the Hebrew word are JHVH. When he wanted to speak of God he used the vowels from another name which means 'Lord'. Because the word was never pronounced and never written with vowels, the vowels became forgotten and it is impossible to know exactly how the name should be pronounced. Scholars are agreed that the most likely pronunciation was JAHVEH and this is the word we shall use in this book to describe Israel's God.

CHAPTER 3

The Division of the Kingdom

To study: I Kings, chapters 11 and 12

The end of the Reign of Solomon
Solomon is remembered in history for his splendour and his wisdom, but there was a darker side to his reign which had more influence on history than all his reputed glory. To secure alliances with other nations he had married many wives. These wives were of different religions, and when they came to Jerusalem they brought with them their own priests and Solomon built for them shrines where they could worship their own gods. This meant that many gods were being worshipped in Jerusalem and probably Solomon himself was not unwilling to share in that worship. We can read what our historian thought about this in the first part of *I Kings* 11.

His magnificence too had a reverse side. Great buildings are not erected without money and without labour. Solomon obtained the money for his projects by heavy taxation, and the labour by demanding three months free labour from every man of his kingdom. Imagine being dragged away from your home for three months of the year to work in some other part of the country at digging in mines or erecting buildings – and all for nothing. No wonder there was growing discontent. The position was not made easier when men saw that however beautiful the new Temple might be, Solomon's palace was much larger and more beautiful, and Solomon himself lived in great luxury. You can get an idea of the luxury by turning up *I Kings* 4 *22-23* and seeing what was eaten at the court in one day! Ominous signs were already present when there were revolts in two parts of the country (I Kings 11 *14* and *23*).

The real discontent, however, centred round Jeroboam. Jeroboam was one of Solomon's task masters in charge of the labour force in the provinces. He is described as a 'mighty man of valour' and 'industrious'. On one occasion when he was out in the country, he was met by the prophet Ahijah*. By a symbolic action (I Kings 11 *29-39*) Ahijah told Jeroboam that he was to be ruler of ten of the tribes of Israel. This story is important because it shows us a prophet interfering in political affairs on behalf of God and the common people. The prophets were the only group of men in the East who represented the common people and were immune from royal punishment owing to their sanctity. We shall have many illustrations of this later but take note of this one, the first in your period.

Solomon must have got wind of the plot centring round Jeroboam, for he tried to kill him. However, Jeroboam got away and fled to Egypt. The Pharaoh there was Shishak*, who was already dreaming of attacking Palestine and who was only too willing to shelter and help any revolutionary. Jeroboam stayed there until Solomon died.

The Disruption

When Solomon died it was the natural thing for his son, Rehoboam, to take his place. He seems to have been accepted by the tribe of Judah and made king in Jerusalem. He knew, however, that the Northern tribes were restive and so he came to meet them and be acclaimed as king in Shechem. Probably he had arranged as a matter of diplomacy to have his coronation in Shechem*. When he arrived there he found the tribes gathered to meet him, and Jeroboam was with them. You can read the story of what happened in *I Kings* 12 *1-17*.

The Northern tribes were quite willing to have Rehoboam as king if he would lighten their burdens; in other words if he would return to the old standards of David. He asked for time to consider. He consulted the old counsellors, who advised him to agree to the demands of the Northern tribes. He then consulted his young friends who advised him to be firmer with them. He took the advice of the young men and refused to lower the taxes, adding to his refusal threats to be even harsher than Solomon.

The reaction was immediate. The people rejected the house of David. 'To your tents, O Israel', was a call for revolt and symbolised the aim of getting back to the simpler days before the luxury of Solomon. Rehoboam fled to Jerusalem and Jeroboam was made king. Rehoboam sent Adoram*, his chief of labour, to bring the rebels to heel but he was unceremoniously lynched (I Kings 12 *18*).

When he returned to Jerusalem, Rehoboam began to make preparations for war against the Northern tribes. Solomon's army was still intact and there is little doubt that he could have subdued Israel with the forces at his command. Once again, however, a prophet interfered. This time Shemaiah* forbade him to take up arms against the North, for God had said, 'This thing is from Me' (I Kings 12 *21-24*). The prophets did not recognise the right of the Davidic dynasty to rule Israel for ever. They represented a desire abroad in Israel to return from the luxury of Solomon's kingdom to a more ancient way of life – if need be, by revolution.

The Kingdom of Israel was divided – never to be reunited. The empire of Solomon collapsed almost overnight. Israel and Judah became two second-rate states existing side by side. Because Jeroboam was of the tribe of Ephraim, the Northern kingdom is sometimes called Ephraim.

From now on we must follow two stories, often intermingled, until first one people and then the other disappears into exile.

Summary   922 BC

Solomon leaves a legacy of bitterness.

Ahijah incites Jeroboam to rebel.

The Northern tribes confront Rehoboam at Shechem.

Rehoboam refuses to ease their burdens.

'To your tents, O Israel' – the kingdom is divided.

Rehoboam is forbidden by Shemaiah to attack the Northern tribes.

Questions

1. Describe how, after the death of Solomon, his kingdom came to be divided. With what justification has Solomon himself been blamed for what happened?

2. Write notes on:

   a. 'and Ahijah caught the new garment that was on him and tore it into twelve pieces.'

   b. 'My father hath chastised you with whips. I will chastise you with scorpions.'

   c. 'To your tents, O Israel! What portion have we in David?'

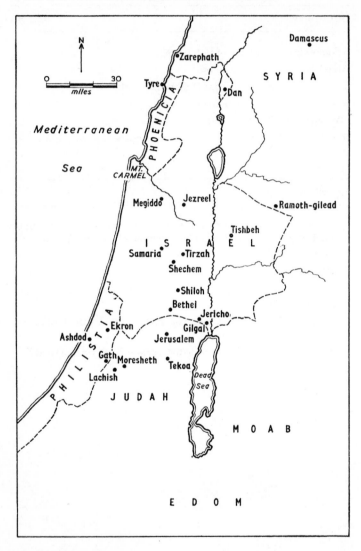

The Kingdoms of Israel and Judah

CHAPTER 4

Jeroboam and his Successors

To study: I Kings 12 *15-33*
　　　　　14 *19-20*
　　　　　16 *1-22*

We turn now to follow the fortunes of the Northern kingdom. Jeroboam began to reign about 922 BC and reigned
for twenty-two years. He had to begin at the very beginning and organise his kingdom from nothing. The first
thing he did was to fortify Shechem and make it his capital
(I Kings 12 *25*). This was a wise choice. It was the place
where Abraham had built his first altar on entering Canaan;
it was centrally situated and was linked with ancient religious practises; it was also loosely linked with the tribal
system and would not be likely to arouse tribal jealousies.
Later the capital was moved to Tirzah, seven miles north-
east of Shechem. Jeroboam also fortified Penuel on the other
side of the Jordan.

The kingdom now had a centre of government but it had
no centre of worship. The Temple at Jerusalem was still
the shrine of the people and many people would still go
there to worship, not seeing anything odd in doing so. But
the main feature of the worship at Jerusalem was the celebration of God's eternal Covenant with David. To allow
his people to be subject to this influence might seriously
undermine their loyalty to the Northern throne. Jeroboam
therefore gave his royal support to two sanctuaries in the

extreme north and south of his country – Dan and Bethel*
– both places of ancient origin. He also made priests who
were 'not of the sons of Levi'*.

Jerusalem, however, still had an advantage. The Ark of
the Covenant which linked directly on to the religion of
Moses was in the Temple. Jeroboam decided that in order
to form a link with the religion of Moses he would erect
bull images of God at his two sancturaries to take the
place of the Ark. This represented a very ancient Northern
Israelite tradition in which God was represented as standing on the back of a young bull. There was no intention of
idolatry. The bulls were intended as pedestals on which the
unseen figure of God rode, just as, in fact, were the cherubim
in the Temple at Jerusalem.

But these bulls were also symbols of the Canaanite fertility cult and there was an obvious danger. See the separate
note at the end of this chapter on 'Canaanite Religion'.

Jeroboam also instituted an annual religious festival in
the eighth month, again to counteract the influence of the
festivals at Jerusalem.

All the writers of the Bible consider that Jeroboam, by
setting up a rival kingdom to that of David, committed the
unforgivable sin. The introduction of the bull images
made him despised and hated by the writer of the history.
He is described throughout the record as 'Jeroboam, the
son of Nebat, who made Israel to sin'. None of his successors
is acquitted of sin.

Jeroboam's Successors

Jeroboam was succeeded by his son Nadab who reigned for
two years before being assassinated by Baasha. Baasha
reigned for twenty-four years but the only important event
from our point of view is an attack he made on Judah in the
reign of Asa, of which we shall read later. His son Elah
reigned for two years before being assassinated by Zimri,
who in turn perished in a palace fire after a reign of only

seven days. The historian can find nothing good to say of any of them and so finishes them off quickly. When Zimri died the captain of the army, Omri, took over the kingdom by a coup d'état and became one of the most powerful kings Israel ever had.

NOTE ON CANAANITE RELIGION

The religion of the Canaanites was a nature religion similar to that in the Fertile Crescent and elsewhere. We get our information about it from the *Ras Shamra** tablets. These were discovered in 1929 at Ras Shamra on the coast of Syria. They date from 1350 bc and give us a clear picture of Canaanite religion and its practices.

Chief among the Canaanite gods was the high god 'El', the 'King, the father of years', and his consort was Asherah. Next in rank was the storm god, Baal*, lord of the gods and creator of mankind. In the ritual poems the chief part is played by Baal, the god of rain and fertility, who takes the form of a bull, the animal of strength and fertility. His consort sister is the warrior goddess Anath, known for violent sexual passion and sadistic brutality.

This was a practical religion for farmers. Baal was the lord of the earth and owner of the land. He could also give fertility to the soil. The fertility powers must be worshipped. The idea was that through the intercourse of the gods the ground became fertile. To get them to give fertility you had to show them what you wanted them to do. This gave rise to all kinds of obscene fertility rites.

From the very beginning this religion had been a real danger to the people of Israel. Coming from the wilderness they sometimes had doubts as to whether their wilderness god, Jahveh, had any control over agricultural processes and they were tempted to be on the safe side and worship Baal to ensure good crops. We shall see that this influence had by no means ceased to be a danger in our period. Imagine, therefore, the horror with which the bull images of Jeroboam were regarded. They not only might be worshipped as idols but might encourage all kinds of evil practices.

Summary   922-876 BC

Jeroboam I *a.* Capital at Shechem and later, Tirzah.

       b. Shrines at Dan and Bethel.

       c. Bull images.

       d. Annual Festival.

       e. He 'makes Israel to sin'.

Nadab

Baasha attacks Asa of Judah.

Elah

Zimri

Omri

Ras Shamra tablets describe Canaanite religion.

Questions

---

1. What problems faced Jeroboam when he came to the throne of Israel and how did he meet them?

2. In what way did Jeroboam, the son of Nebat, 'make Israel to sin'?

3. Write an outline account of the events of the reign of Jeroboam, son of Nebat.

CHAPTER 5

Rehoboam and his Successors

To study: I Kings 14 *21-31*
              15 *1-24*

In the Southern kingdom of Judah, Rehoboam succeeded Solomon his father and reigned for seven years.
There were in Jerusalem and Judah two important groups
of people. On the one hand were the aristocracy who had
been prosperous in the days of Solomon and who wished
things to continue as they were. They were international
in their outlook and tolerant in their attitude to religion,
with little feeling for the religion of the early days which
had demanded complete loyalty to Jahveh. On the other
hand, there was the rural population consisting mainly of
small farmers and shepherds who clung to the ancient
social and religious traditions. During the reigns of Rehoboam and Abijah, the aristocratic, tolerant party held the
upper hand and the paganising tendencies begun and encouraged by Solomon continued.

Rehoboam 922-915
We are told that Rehoboam frequented the local sanctuaries with their Canaanitish practices. These included obscene rites of worship, prostitution and homosexuality. For
this he is roundly condemned by the historian.

He also struggled to hold the Benjamin territory which
bordered on Judah to the north because it was close to his

capital. This accounts for the sporadic warfare which seems to have continued between Judah and Israel.

The chief event of the reign is noted as the invasion by Shishak, king of Egypt. Shishak was determined to reassert Egyptian power and authority in Palestine. This is why he had given refuge to Jeroboam, hoping that a revolutionary would split and weaken the kingdom. About the year 918 he struck into Palestine with great force. The Biblical account seems to suggest that the attack was against Jerusalem alone. However, Shishak's own inscriptions survive at Karnak in Egypt and these list over a hundred and fifty places in Judah and Israel which he claimed to have taken. As far north as Megiddo a fragment of a triumphal stele, a stone column recording Shishak's victories, has been found. It is clear that he devastated nearly all Palestine and pressed at least as far as Esdraelon.

Rehoboam had to pay an enormous tribute and Shishak took away the treasures of the Temple, including the shields of gold which Solomon had made. Rehoboam substituted shields of brass because he could not afford to replace them with gold.

Shishak was unable to follow up his conquest because Egypt was internally weak and trouble at home caused him to withdraw from Palestine.

Abijah 915-913

Rehoboam was succeeded by his son Abijah (or Abijam). Nothing of importance occurred in his short reign except that the frontier fighting continued. There is a story in *II Chronicles* 13 which describes one of the battles in which Abijah defeated Jeroboam of Israel.

Asa 913-873

The coming of Asa to the throne meant a change in the direction of religious policy. Asa swept away the immoralities and idols from Judah and freed her officially from the pagan cults. He also removed the queen mother, Maacah*, from her official position because she worshipped an Asherah*, which he burned. (An Asherah was a kind of wooden pole which represented the goddess in the Canaanite religion.) He receives high praise from the historian although it is noted that 'the high places* were not taken away.'

A reference to Asa in *II Chronicles* 14 says that he repulsed an Ethiopian army at Mareshah, but the chief event of his reign from an international point of view was the attack that Baasha of Israel made upon him (I Kings 15 *16-22*).

Baasha marched against Judah and began to fortify Ramah*, a small town only five miles north of Jerusalem. Asa was desperate as he saw the fortifications being prepared against him and appealed to Benhadad I*, king of Syria, to help him. Benhadad had a treaty with Israel, but the opportunity to interfere in the affairs of Israel and Judah was too good to miss. The fact that Asa supported his appeal with a substantial gift from the Temple treasury no doubt helped Benhadad to decide (II Chron 16). He broke his treaty with Israel and attacked Galilee, thus forcing Baasha to withdraw from attacking Judah to defend his own borders. With the withdrawal of Baasha Asa dismantled the fortifications at Ramah and strengthened his own frontiers. Asa was later condemned by the prophet Hanani for his lack of faith in God (II Chron 16).

Summary	922-873 BC

Rehoboam *a.* Frequents local sanctuaries.

b. Constant warfare with Israel.

c. Invasion by Shishak of Egypt.

Abijah (or Abijam)

Asa *a.* Sweeps away pagan cults.

b. Appeals to Syria when Israel attacks.

c. Strengthens frontiers.

Questions

1. Write an account of the reign of Rehoboam up to the time of his death.

2. Write notes on: Shishak; Benhadad I; Abijah.

CHAPTER 6

Omri and Ahab

To study: I Kings 16 *23* to 22 *40*

Omri 876-869

As we have seen in Chapter 4, Omri took the throne of Israel by a coup d'état. The leader of the army was in a powerful position under the confused conditions of the time. But Omri proved a wise and far-sighted ruler and has sometimes been described as a 'Northern David'. Only six verses are given by the Biblical writer to describe his reign but that gives no idea of his real achievements. He established a dynasty of such prestige that the Assyrians referred to Israel as the 'land of Omri' for many years after his death and the downfall of his dynasty.

Omri was faced with very real problems. The first was the continued pressure of his northern neighbour, Syria. Benhadad I was a great ruler and he was determined to reach the sea coast with his armies. He had taken advantage of Israel's weakness to annex certain border towns. Omri managed to keep Syria at bay but only by giving up some territory in Transjordan* and granting the Syrians concessions in commercial relations with Samaria (I Kings 20 *34*).

The second and even greater danger was the rising power of Assyria. Under Ashur-nasir-pal II she overran Mesopotamia and pursued a policy of great brutality. She reached the coast at Tyre and Sidon before withdrawing and now presented a constant danger to the smaller countries of Palestine.

Omri began to build a new capital. He fortified Samaria, which had a very strong natural position and could be defended fairly easily. Archaeologists have discovered the remains of Omri's fortifications and palaces and declare that they represent the finest building before the Roman period.

He now had to enter into alliances in order to strengthen himself against possible attack from Assyria. To make an alliance with the Phoenicians, the greatest trading power in the world of the day, he arranged a marriage between his son, Ahab, and Jezebel, princess of Tyre. He then sought an alliance with Judah, so he arranged another marriage, between Athaliah and Jehoram, the king of Judah. There is some doubt as to who Athaliah was. In *II Kings* 8 *18* she is described as the daughter of Ahab; in *II Kings* 8 *26* as the daughter of Omri (although R.S.V. has 'granddaughter'). Since Athaliah's son was born about 864 BC she could not have been the daughter of Ahab and Jezebel, who had only been married ten years at the time. She was probably Ahab's half-sister or a daughter born to Ahab before Omri came to the throne and before Ahab was married to Jezebel. She was, at any rate, a daughter of the house of Omri and her marriage to Jehoram ended the feud between Israel and Judah.

Omri was determined to secure all his frontiers and to complete this work he attacked and conquered Moab. The Moabite Stone, now in the Louvre in Paris, was erected by the king of Moab, Mesha, and on it are the words 'Omri afflicted the land of Moab many days' – a record of the attack from outside our Biblical sources.

There is no doubt that, despite the small space given to him in the Bible, Omri was a great king, wise in diplomacy, and he gave Israel a security she had not known for years.

Ahab 869-850
Omri was succeeded by Ahab and to him the Biblical

writer gives considerable space because he was very important for religion. During his reign the great issue came to be decided – was Israel to go forward on the path that led to monotheism* (the worship of one God) or was she to relapse into polytheism* (the worship of many gods)?

On the political side, Ahab's reign was dominated by the struggle with Syria and the threat of Assyria. Assyria's king, Ashur-nasir-pal, had been succeeded by Shalmaneser III and he launched an attack towards the Mediterranean coasts. The kings of the West formed a coalition against him and to this coalition Ahab of Israel contributed 2,000 chariots and 10,000 foot soldiers. According to the annals of Shalmaneser himself this was the largest number of chariots contributed by any of the allies.

The allied kings met Shalmaneser at Qarqar on the Orontes in 853. Shalmaneser boasted that he gained a great victory. It could hardly have been as great as he claimed, for he immediately withdrew and it was five years before he was ready to attack again. Nevertheless the attack towards the sea was a shadow of things to come. From that time on Assyria remained the greatest threat.

We shall look at Ahab's relations with Syria later for it was in a clash with Syria that he finally lost his life. The greatest influence in Ahab's reign was his marriage to Jezebel. Jezebel came from Tyre in Phoenicia and had the Eastern idea of absolute monarchy – the king could do as he liked. There was no question of his being just God's representative. She was also a worshipper of Baal. When a princess came to live in another country it was only natural that she should want to worship her own god. Solomon had provided shrines for his many wives to do just this. Jezebel insisted on doing the same but she did it on a grand scale. She brought with her the Tyrian religion. She erected an altar for Baal, made an Asherah and brought with her a large number of priests of the cult. We are told that she brought 400 priests and 850 prophets. Obviously these were for a larger purpose than just to enable her to worship her own god. She started a campaign for converts. Prophets of Jahveh now faced reprisals for speaking the word of God. Many yielded to her influence and spoke only what the king and queen wished to hear. Others refused to compromise and faced the consequences.

Along with this deterioration of religion, social conditions had changed for the worse. There was wealth in the country but it was concentrated in the hands of the few. The lot of the peasantry had deteriorated and the poor came to be at the mercy of the rich. The story of Naboth's vineyard was probably not an isolated case.

Two protest movements begin to be seen at this time. Both of them protest against the settled life of the town and at the same time plead for a return to the more simple conditions of the wilderness. The Nazirites were never a revolutionary group although they refused to drink wine and kept themselves separate. The Rechabites*, however, were definitely a revolutionary group aiming to restore the conditions of the nomad age. They were founded by Jonadab (or Jehonadab) the son of Rechab. They refused to drink wine, till fields or live in solid houses. Jonadab* himself was the head of a family devoted to the traditions of the wilderness in opposition to the agricultural ways of Canaan. He was a descendant of the Kenites or Midianites, the nomads who influenced and supported Moses in the wilderness. You should be able to write notes on the Rechabites and for this purpose you will need to include two passages which we shall look at later, viz. *II Kings* 10 *15-17*; *Jeremiah* 35.

The Coming of Elijah

Against this background we have to see the coming of Elijah. He was one of the greatest of all the prophets. In himself he is a strange figure. He has a miraculous gift of hiding. He appears suddenly as if from nowhere and vanishes just as suddenly. In the end he vanishes into the desert.

His God was the God of Sinai who would have no rival and would exact blood vengeance for crimes against the Covenant law such as Ahab and Jezebel had committed. He declared Holy War against the pagan state and the god it was worshipping. The Elijah stories are to be found in *I Kings* 17, 18, 19, and 21. We shall look at each in turn.

a. I Kings 17. Read the chapter carefully. Elijah announces Jahveh as God of the Land. This is against the Canaanite and Phoenician belief that Baal is god of the land and controls fertility. Elijah is concerned to show that Jahveh has authority over the fertility of the land and all men are in his hands. He announces a drought to come and the sufferings that will follow it. He himself goes to the brook Cherith, where he is fed by ravens. Later he goes to Zarephath. Now Zarephath is in Phoenicia and the drought is there too – God not only controls conditions in Israel but in the stronghold of Baal himself. Read carefully the story of the widow of Zarephath. It is similar in some respects to the story of Elisha and the woman of Shunem. Be careful not to get the details mixed up in case you have to tell one of these stories.

b. I Kings 18. Elijah meets Obadiah, one of the king's household, who is also a devotee of Jahveh. Notice Obadiah's reference to Elijah's habit of appearing and disappearing. He says that if he goes to bring his master, by the time he gets back Elijah might have disappeared!

We now get the story of the contest on Mount Carmel. Read it carefully and note the details. Carmel is chosen because it is on the high road to Phoenicia. Elijah is carrying the war into the enemy's camp. He challenges the people, 'How long halt ye between two opinions?' Literally we should translate, 'How long hop ye on two branches?' The picture is that of a bird hopping along a branch until it comes to a fork. It can't decide which way to go and so it tries to go along keeping one foot on each side of the fork. The challenge is – one God or many? You can't take both positions. Notice the sarcasm as Elijah taunts the prophets of Baal. Israel has come to the fork in the road and Elijah, in one of the most dramatic scenes in all literature, thunders out the issue.

We will not go into the detail of the story. You must study the text itself, as we have said before, and make a summary of it. For the moment it looks as though Elijah has won. Ahab and the people shout, 'The Lord, He is God.' The rain is coming. Ahab has to rush back to Jezreel before Esdraelon becomes a quagmire. Elijah runs before his chariot whilst the people continue to shout 'Jahveh is God' as they see the rain coming.

c. I Kings 19. But Elijah has reckoned without Jezebel. She stands firm and threatens the prophet, so he runs away. He comes to Horeb (another name for Sinai), the place where the Covenant was first made. Here he thinks it must end. This is the place where a nation pledged itself to God and only one believer is left – 'It is finished.' But God is not defeated. Carmel is not the way. God is not only a God of wonders. Elijah broods on the mountain and the scenes of Moses' day pass before him. Earthquake, wind and fire – God is not now in these. Then a 'still small voice', or better as the R.V. translates, 'a sound of gentle stillness' when nothing seems to be happening. When God seems to be doing nothing, He is working. He is not only the God of wonders – he is the God of the ordinary and of history. He is already preparing judgment. Israel's faith has to find expression in action and not in contemplation. Jahveh acts in history and calls on Elijah to take part in his plan of action. He is told to anoint Jehu king of Israel; in other words, to stir up a revolution. He is also to anoint Hazael king of Syria – God has plans for other nations besides Israel. He is not limited to one people. Jehu will destroy the house of Ahab and Hazael will be God's whip to chastise Israel. There are three great things to notice here: (i) Jahveh is no longer just a national god; (ii) He

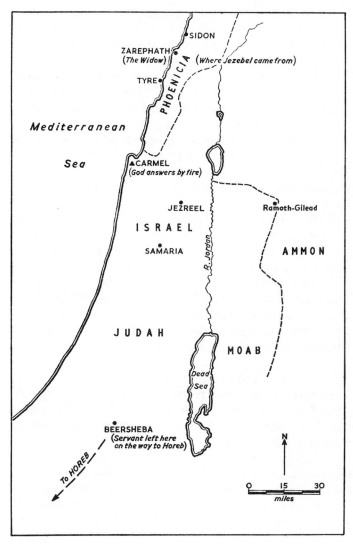

Places visited by Elijah

works in history; (iii) the beginning of the doctrine of the remnant – there are still seven thousand loyal souls in Israel. When God is deserted by the many He will save by the few.

d. I Kings 21. This is the story of Naboth's vineyard, which you should read carefully. The Israelite view was that Jahveh was the owner of the land. Families acted as his stewards as they had possession of it. This is not Naboth's property merely – it is a family estate. When Naboth refuses to sell, Ahab realises that nothing more can be done. He has no thoughts of violating the rights of the peasant. To the queen, however, there is no problem. The king should have what he wants and she works her scheme to that end. Elijah sees it as murder and Jahveh is the guardian of the helpless. The remarkable thing in the story is not that a king should take a vineyard – any Eastern monarch would have done the same. The remarkable thing is that a prophet should be found to rebuke him. The conflict now is not just about worship. It has to do with questions of right and wrong and the relationships between people. The Mosaic Covenant has demands which go beyond Church services to the whole of life.

Ahab's Wars with Syria

There are two chapters to consider here. In *I Kings* 20 Ahab has two battles with Benhadad of Syria and defeats him. Read this chapter carefully and notice the details of the story. There is a year between the two battles. Notice also that the Syrians think they have been defeated the first time because Israel's God is 'a god of the hills and not of the valleys'. After the battle of Aphek, Ahab treats Benhadad with remarkable leniency. This was probably a wise move from the point of view of diplomacy but it disgusted some of the prophets.

The second story in *I Kings* 22 is a very important one. We remember that when Omri made his peace with Syria he had to give up certain towns. One of these was Ramoth-Gilead*, an important commercial and strategic centre. After the battle of Aphek, Ahab makes it a condition of peace that Ramoth-Gilead should be returned. Benhadad is unwilling to part with it so Ahab decides that it is time to take it by force. He invites Jehoshaphat, king of Judah, to join with him in the expedition. Jehoshaphat accepts the invitation but insists that a word should be sought from God as to whether it is His will. One cannot help thinking that Jehoshaphat is not very eager to go and hopes that the prophetic oracle will forbid the venture. Ahab calls the four hundred prophets who are in the pay of the Court and they immediately say, 'Go up and prosper'. They are 'Yes' men and are paid to say that Jahveh's will coincides with Ahab's wishes. But the Judean king is suspicious. Is there not another prophet? Ahab says that there is one – Micaiah* – but he never has a good word to say about Ahab. However, he is called. Imagine him entering the presence of the two kings with the prophets surrounding him. He is told that it is the unanimous verdict of the four hundred that Ahab shall go to Ramoth-Gilead. What shall he say? At first he sarcastically agrees with the prophets. Ahab wants to go. His mind is made up – so why dissuade him? But Ahab now puts him on oath to say what God is speaking. He says he sees Israel without a leader and the expedition a failure. He also sees Jahveh filling the other prophets with lies. The leader of the four hundred strikes Micaiah and Ahab puts him in prison. Ahab goes to Ramoth-Gilead as he wants to do and takes what precautions he can, but he is accidentally wounded and dies.

The great point here is that prophecy is no longer the mere echo of nationalism or the king's wishes. In Elijah and Micaiah we find men who are prepared to speak the word of God whatever the cost. This is a break with the professional prophets and the beginning of a trend which is to influence Israel in the days to come.

Summary   876-850 BC

Omri   *a.* Gives up territory to Syria.

      b. New capital at Samaria.

      c. Forms alliance with Phoenicia by marriage of Ahab to Jezebel.

      d. Forms alliance with Judah by marriage of Athaliah to Jehoram.

      e. The Moabite stone records his victories there.

Ahab   *a.* Contributes to the coalition against Assyria. Qarqar.

      b. Jezebel introduces Baal worship.

      c. Social conditions decline.

      d. The Nazirites and the Rechabites.

      e. War with Benhadad.

      f. Ramoth-Gilead and Micaiah.

Elijah   *a.* The famine and the widow of Zarephath.

      b. The contest on Carmel.

      c. Elijah goes to Horeb.

      d. Naboth's vineyard.

Questions

1. What problems did Omri face on coming to the throne and how did he deal with them?

2. Write a full account of the seizure of Naboth's vineyard by Ahab and Jezebel, showing in your account how four of the Ten Commandments were broken by the king and queen.

3. Why did Elijah flee to Horeb? What happened while he was there? What commands did he receive from God while he was there?

4. What results followed in Israel from the marriage between Ahab and Jezebel in so far as Israel's religious life was concerned? What, in general, was the role played by the prophet Elijah in this situation?

5. What was the significance for Israel's religious and political life of Elijah's struggle and achievements?

The Chart so far

Important Kings in italics

Egypt	Judah	Israel	Syria	Mesopotamia
900 BC	*Rehoboam*	*Jeroboam I*		
Shishak—→				
	Abijah			
		Nadab		
	Asa ←———	Baasha ←——	*Benhadad I*	
		Elah		
		Zimri		
		Omri		
	Jehoshaphat			*Shalmaneser III* (Battle of Qarqar)
850 BC		*Ahab* ———→		
		Ramoth-Gilead		

N.B. The arrows indicate invasions.

CHAPTER 7

Israel and Judah after Ahab

To study: I Kings 22 *41-50*
II Kings 1 to 9

The Successors of Ahab

Ahab was succeeded by *Ahaziah* (850-849), who has no significance except that he fell through a window and died (II Kings 1). He was followed by *Jehoram* (849-842) (II Kings 3).

About this time we have the story of the passing of Elijah and his being succeeded by Elisha. Read carefully the story in *II Kings 2*. When Elijah was about to depart Elisha asked him for a 'double portion' of his spirit. This was the portion of a man's property which was allowed to his eldest son and marked him as the man's heir. When Elisha asked for this double portion of Elijah's spirit, he was asking to be recognised as Elijah's true successor. Elijah said that he would receive it if he saw him depart, whereupon Elisha determined not to leave Elijah. He did see the departure and as Elijah was taken away, he cried, 'The chariots of Israel and the horsemen thereof.' By this he meant that Elijah had been to the nation a greater defence than horses and chariots and that Israel had suffered a great loss.

In Chapter 3 we have the story of the reign of Jehoram. He removed some of the objects of the pagan cult in order to appease the prophetic supporters but he could not go very far in any reformation for Jezebel was still alive and a power in the land. His aunt, Athaliah, was the wife of

Jehoram, king of Judah, so that the house of Omri was still dominant in both Northern and Southern kingdoms.

The most important event of Jehoram's reign from our point of view was his attack on Moab. Mesha, king of Moab, had been a vassal of Ahab, providing him annually with 100,000 lambs and the wool of 100,000 rams. He took the opportunity afforded by the change in Israel's kingship to rebel and Jehoram attempted to subdue him. He attacked Moab, assisted by the kings of Judah and Edom. The attack nearly ended in disaster when the armies failed to find water where they had expected. Elisha was called in, with the result that a sudden cloudburst filled the stream. The Moabites, seeing the sun's reflection upon the water, thought that the allies had fallen out and shed each other's blood. The Moabites therefore advanced out of the city and were routed. As a last desperate measure the king of Moab offered up his son as a sacrifice on the city walls. When the attackers saw this they were horrified and fled in panic.

According to the Moabite Stone, Mesha then advanced into Israel across the river Arnon and massacred the Israelites and settled Moabites in their place.

There was constant border warfare with Damascus during the reign of Jehoram; in fact, the armies of Israel and Syria were still locked in battle at Ramoth-Gilead after eight years.

The Prophets

We now need to look at a phenomenon which comes into the story quite frequently in our period. This is the rise of the so-called 'prophets' or 'Nebi'im' as they were called. We first come into contact with them in the days of Samuel where they appear to be bands of Jahveh enthusiasts who had formed themselves into guilds. Their chief characteristic was ecstasy. They worked themselves up into a frenzy and indulged in violent contortions and frantic dances. The 'dancing dervishes' of the East would be a modern parallel. They worked themselves into a frenzy by music. The frenzy was explained by saying that the 'spirit of the Lord' had come upon them. Frequently in the early days their purpose was to work up popular enthusiasm for war against the Philistines. They wandered about in bands from place to place although quite often they seem to have been based upon a centre, e.g. there were bands of prophets associated with Gilgal, Bethel and Jericho.

This phenomenon was not limited to Israel. It was quite common elsewhere and we remember the prophets of Baal whipping themselves into a frenzy and cutting themselves with knives on Mount Carmel.

We find, however, that when a special word of God is needed, the message comes to an individual. He may be a member of a prophetic group; in fact, it is probable that originally Nathan, Elijah and Elisha belonged to one of these groups. When the word came, however, the individual came out from the group and pursued his own path.

To begin with, the prophets were very popular and as the priesthood became corrupt, people began to rely more and more on the prophets to give the authentic word of God. But as time passed they tended to become 'professional' and no longer claimed to have had a genuine 'call'. They went about for what they could get in the way of financial rewards and deliberately courted popularity. Many became no more than hangers-on at court prepared to prophesy what the ruler wanted provided they were well paid. We have already had an example of this in the story of the four hundred prophets who encouraged Ahab to go to Ramoth-Gilead because they knew he wanted to go. Some of the prophets indulged in sorcery and were branded as 'false prophets'.

In our story we have several references to these prophets. You will have noticed that when Elijah and Elisha journey together before Elijah is taken away, at various places they meet the prophets who are obviously living in community and who tell Elisha that his master is to be taken away. They seem sometimes to be grouped around a leader or master (II Kings 6 *1-7*). Their dress was distinguishable, too – Elijah is recognised because 'he wore a garment of haircloth with a girdle of leather about his loins'. Sometimes they gave their oracles in groups, as the four hundred did to Ahab, and sometimes singly as when Elisha prophesied rain in Moab. It seems that a fee was usually expected for their work. The story of Gehazi and Naaman implies that Naaman expected to pay a fee for Elisha's services (II Kings 5 *15-16*). They were often thought mad and we shall notice that Jehu described one of them as 'this mad fellow' (II Kings 9 *11*).

In general, the prophets were great patriots urging people to fight for their country and their God. They supported the wars against Syria from a patriotic motive. Above all at this time they were violently opposed to the house of Omri and all that it stood for. We shall find Elisha working in close contact with these groups of prophets.

The Elisha Stories

In Chapters 1 to 9 of II Kings we have a collection of stories about Elisha. They are not told in chronological order, but are placed together to give a picture of the work of Elijah's successor. Elisha led the opposition to the house of Omri as Elijah had done before him and, as we have seen, worked in close co-operation with the prophetic orders. The stories of Elisha are mainly of miracle and contain much legend. They show him to be a very different man from Elijah. Where Elijah was an austere man who startled everyone by his sudden comings and goings, Elisha was a man of the Court, living with his fellows and showing great concern and compassion for them. The stories reveal his character and show the impression that he made.

45

You should read these chapters carefully and make a special note of those to which we now draw your attention.

In Chapter 4 Elisha's concern for the relatives of one of the prophets is shown and this is followed by the story of the woman of Shunem. This story is somewhat similar to the story of Elijah's encounter with the widow of Zarephath, but there are important differences. Notice carefully the differences between the two stories and be able to relate them in fair detail.

In Chapter 5 the well-known story of Naaman occurs. The background to this story is the border warfare which constantly goes on between Syria and Israel. On one of the raids across the border the Syrians have taken captives and one of them, a young girl, is taken to be the maid of Naaman's wife. Read the story carefully and beware of thinking that you know it because it is so familiar. You should note particularly two points concerning verse *17*. When Naaman leaves Elisha he asks for two mules' burden of earth to take back with him to Syria. He is grateful to Israel's God, in fact, he says that he now knows there is no God except in Israel and he wants to worship Israel's God when he gets back home. He believes, however, that a god can only be worshipped on the soil of his own country. Accordingly, he takes some Israelitish soil back to Syria so that he can stand or kneel upon it and worship Israel's God. He also points out to Elisha that his official duties demand that he goes into the temple of Rimmon with his master, the king of Syria, on official occasions. He asks forgiveness in advance for these occasions – giving the impression that he will only be going as a formality and not as an act of worship.

Chapter 6 describes another Syrian attack upon Israel. The point of it is to emphasise the hidden resources that are at Elisha's disposal because he is a man of God.

Chapter 8 is important. You will remember that on Mt. Horeb Elijah had been given three tasks. He was to anoint Jehu to be king over Israel, Hazael to be king over Syria

and Elisha to be his successor as prophet. He had only fulfilled the last task of the three, the other two tasks were
left for Elisha to accomplish. In verses *7* to *15* of Chapter 8
Elisha journeys to Damascus. Whilst he is there, the king of
Syria, Benhadad, who is suffering from sickness, sends one
of his officers, Hazael, to enquire from Elisha if he will recover. Elisha replies that the king will recover from his
sickness but that nevertheless he will die. He says that
Hazael will be the next king of Syria and will bring calamity
to Israel. Hazael returned and the next day he murdered
Benhadad and seized the throne.

Kings of Judah

We have already heard of *Jehoshaphat* (873-849) who went
to fight with Ahab at Ramoth-Gilead. He seems to have
been subject to Ahab for the greater part of his reign. His
military alliance with Ahab brought strength and prosperity to Judah. He was too loyal a worshipper of Jahveh
to allow the Baal religion to come from Israel into Judah
and he sought to suppress all pagan practices.

He asserted his authority over Edom. There is a long
account of his reign in *II Chronicles* 17 to 20 which is likely
to be fairly correct. He evidently undertook defensive
measures and a great judicial reform. There were to be
royally appointed judges in key cities and a court of
appeal in Jerusalem.

There seems also to have been an attempt to reopen the
sea-port at Ezion-geber* on the Gulf of Aqaba but the
ships of Tarshish* which were meant to go to Ophir for
gold were wrecked (I Kings 22 *47-49*).

Jehoshaphat was succeeded by Jehoram (849-842), who
reigned at the same time as a king of Israel of the same
name. He was the one who married Athaliah and she dominated her husband in all things throughout his life. She
introduced the cult of Baal into Jerusalem. According to
II Chronicles 21 *2-4*, Jehoram put to death all his brothers

47

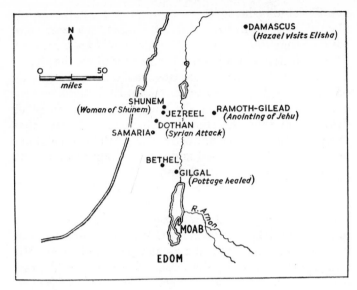

Places visited by Elisha

to get rid of any rival for the throne, and he was probably encouraged by his wife to do this. During his reign Edom revolted and became independent. Judah thus lost some valuable mines and an outlet to the sea at Ezion-geber.

From our point of view Jehoram is not very important. The dominant figure is that of Athaliah, his wife, and she also dominated her son, Ahaziah (842), who succeeded his father to the throne.

Summary   850-842 BC

Israel Ahaziah

Jehoram   *a.* The coming of Elisha.

b. Makes some reform.

c. Attacks Moab.

The coming of the prophets.

Elisha   *a.* The woman of Shunem.

b. Naaman.

c. Syrian attack.

d. Anointing of Hazael.

Judah **Jehoshaphat** *a.* Alliance with Ahab.

b. Puts down pagan practices.

c. Asserts authority over Edom.

d. Judicial reforms.

Jehoram   Influenced by Athaliah. Loses Edom.

Questions

1. Relate the story of Naaman, the Syrian leper-captain, and explain the meaning of the 'two mules' burden of earth'.

2. Write an account of the scene in which the prophet Elijah takes leave of his successor, Elisha.

CHAPTER 8

Revolution

To study: II Kings 8 to 12

The Revolution
Jehoram of Israel and Ahaziah of Judah had joined together as Ahab and Jehoshaphat had done, to recover Ramoth-Gilead from Syria. Jehoram was wounded in battle and retired to Jezreel to recover. While he was there, he was visited by Ahaziah.

At home, forces were massing against them both because they were members of the house of Omri. The prophets were opposed to all that the family of Omri stood for. In addition to the work of Elijah and Elisha, the bands of wandering prophets were stirring up the people against the worship of Baal.

There was dissatisfaction in the army because of the long-drawn-out war with Syria.

Among the ruling classes there was extreme luxury and decadence which went alongside poverty among the ordinary people. Injustice was rife. The story of Naboth's vineyard was obviously no isolated instance.

Groups of extremists, such as the Rechabites, were spreading discontent.

When the revolution came it was the explosion of pent-up popular anger against the house of Omri and its entire policy.

It was Elisha who supplied the match to start the blaze. He sent one of the prophetic band to anoint as king, Jehu, an army commander fighting at Ramoth-Gilead, thus completing the task given to Elijah on Mt. Horeb. When the army heard of this, they rallied round Jehu and hailed him as king. So that no news of the anointing could reach the ears of the king, Jehu hurried to Jezreel.

The story of his ride to Jezreel is one of the great dramatic chapters of the Bible (II Kings 9). Jehu was brutal and ruthless. At all costs the house of Omri had to go. He killed Jehoram at Jezreel and wounded Ahaziah who fled and died at Megiddo*. Jehu ordered Jehoram's body to be thrown into Naboth's vineyard. At Jezreel he also disposed of Jezebel. The story of her death is horrible but magnificent. The character of Jezebel is revealed. She would not cringe before Jehu. She would die like a queen. So she used her cosmetics as though for a great audience and her last word was the word 'Murderer'.

Jehu then hurried to Samaria where he indulged in an orgy of blood. The whole family of Ahab was exterminated, the priests of Baal were butchered and the temple destroyed (II Kings 10). At Samaria, Jehu also slaughtered a court delegation from Jerusalem. This marked the end of the rival cult and the worship of Jahveh was restored.

An interesting incident is told in Chapter 10. Jehu met Jonadab, the founder of the Rechabites, and invited him into his chariot to 'see my zeal for the Lord'. Jonadab rode with Jehu and thus showed his approval of the purge on behalf of the Rechabites and others who wanted a return to the simple life.

The story of Jehu's revolution is a horrible story of bloodshed. It has been said that 'Jehu is as ugly a figure as Jezebel but the principles he stood for were the only ones that could endure.' He sincerely believed that he was carrying out the religious revolution inspired by the prophets, although he never hesitated to use deceit and murder as his weapons. The horror was not forgotten. Later Hosea was appalled by it and pronounced judgment upon it.

51

From a religious point of view the revolution was an advance. Despite the brutality of Jehu, it meant the end of Baal worship and the restoration of the worship of the one God in Israel. Politically, however, it was a disaster. The purge had removed the ablest of the ruling classes. The murder of Jezebel had destroyed the alliance with Phoenicia and the murder of Ahaziah had alienated Judah. Isolated from allies, Israel was wide open to attack. Jehu had weakened the country and began his reign with few able administrators and no allies.

The Reaction in Judah (II Kings 11)

Athaliah, the queen mother, heard of the murder of her son, Ahaziah. Like Jezebel, she was determined and ruthless. Not merely was her son dead, but her own position and power were threatened. She murdered all the male members of the Davidic family and seized the throne herself in 842. But one member of the royal house, Joash, a young boy, was rescued and hidden for six years by the priest, Jehoiada, and his wife. Meanwhile Athaliah introduced the worship of Baal and carried on the policy of the house of Omri. When Joash was seven years old, he was brought out by Jehoiada and presented to the royal guard. He won their support. The city could not stand against the guard and Joash was proclaimed king. Athaliah, hearing shouts, came to see what was happening. She could only cry 'Treason, Treason', before she was killed. Joash was welcomed by the people, who were glad to be rid of Athaliah, who had been no legitimate ruler in their eyes.

It is interesting to note that whereas in Israel the revolution was inspired by the prophets, in Judah it was inspired and carried through by the priests.

Joash (837-800) now became king. He began his long reign by reaffirming the Covenant and he seems to have been an able administrator. He collected money for the repair of the Temple and when he saw the work was not being done he insisted that the repairs be carried out (II Kings 12).

Hazael invaded southern Palestine as far as Gath in Philistia. He would undoubtedly have marched on Jerusalem if Joash had not used the treasures of the Temple to purchase his safety.

According to the book of *Chronicles* (II Chronicles 24), Joash was a godly king so long as he was under Jehoiada's influence, but his godliness lasted only so long as Jehoiada lived. After Jehoiada's death he fell under more tolerant pagan influences and made himself bitterly disliked until at last he was assassinated. No explanation of the assassination is given in the book of *Kings* but *II Chronicles* 24 says that after the death of Jehoiada, Joash had a quarrel with Jehoiada's son, Zechariah, who was assassinated on the king's orders. If this story is true, it is likely that some partisans of Jehoiada's family determined that Joash should die.

Summary   842-800 BC

Israel   The causes of revolution:

    a. Prophets opposed to house of Omri.

    b. Discontent in the army.

    c. Luxury contrasts with poverty.

    d. Injustice prevalent.

    e. Extremists spread discontent.

The Revolution:

    a. Elisha sends to anoint Jehu.

    b. Jehu rides to Jezreel.

    c. Butchery at Jezreel and Samaria.

    d. Jonadab joins Jehu.

    e. A religious triumph and a political disaster.

Judah   Reaction to the Revolution:

    a. Athaliah seizes the throne.

    b. Joash is saved by Jehoiada.

    c. Athaliah continues policy of house of Omri.

    d. Joash produced and Athaliah murdered.

Joash *a.* Renews Covenant.

    b. Collects money and repairs Temple.

    c. Pays tribute to Hazael.

    d. Good whilst Jehoiada lives.

Questions

1. 'The revolution in Israel was the work of the prophets and that in Judah the work of the priests.' Discuss this statement.

2. What were the main causes of Jehu's revolt?

Palestine during the time of the Syrian conquest, 850-800 BC

CHAPTER 9

The Dynasty of Jehu

To study: II Kings 10 *29-36*, 13, 14 *23-29*

The dynasty of Jehu lasted for a hundred years. The first half of the period was a time of adversity for Israel and the latter half a time of prosperity. This was largely because of the relations between Syria and Assyria. During the reigns of Jehu and Jehoahaz, Syria dominated Israel. In 803 Damascus was made a tributary of Assyria and therefore Syria could not attack Israel.

Jehu 842-815

Jehu's reign was a period of weakness. The purge had left Israel completely paralysed. As we have seen, the murder of Jezebel and the attack on Baal worship had brought the Phoenician alliance to an end. The murder of Ahaziah had broken the alliance with Judah. Israel had lost her material prosperity and her allies at a single stroke.

Hazael, king of Syria, was quick to take advantage of this weakness and he swept into Israel east of Jordan. In 841 Jehu, realising his weakness, put himself under the protection of Assyria by paying tribute to Shalmaneser III. This event is not recorded in the Bible but a picture on the Black Obelisk of Shalmaneser depicts Jehu kneeling before Shalmaneser, who is described as 'the mighty king, king of the universe, king without a rival'. The inscription records that:

'from Jehu, son of Omri, I received silver, gold, a golden saplu-bowl, a golden vase with pointed bottom, golden tumblers, golden buckets, tin, and a staff fit for a king.'

Shalmaneser attacked and laid siege to Damascus. He ravaged it and then pushed on to the Phoenician coast, taking tribute from Tyre and Sidon on the way. He afterwards withdrew and no further attack came from Assyria until the end of the century. Jehu was not to receive any practical help from Shalmaneser. Hazael now had a free hand. He was not pressed by Assyria for Assyria was fully occupied defending other frontiers and so he could concentrate his attention on extending his borders. He managed to take the whole of Transjordan* from Israel.

So far as internal affairs were concerned Jehu was again at a disadvantage. The purge of the ruling classes had robbed the nation of the best of its leaders. A bitterness had been created which split the country for many years. These were the conditions under which he began his reign. Unfortunately he himself possessed neither the understanding nor the ability to master the conditions. He ended the cult of Baal but he was no real devotee of Jahveh. The bull images at Dan and Bethel* were not removed. Pagan practices were left alone. He took no steps to correct the social and economic abuses of the family of Omri. In short, although Baal-worship was officially dead, the fortunes of Israel were at a very low ebb.

Jehoahaz 815-801

The decline continued under Jehoahaz; indeed, for most of the time Israel was little more than a tributary of Syria. Jehoahaz was beaten and the final insult was when Hazael restricted his forces to a bodyguard of ten chariots and fifty horsemen, plus a police force of ten thousand footmen. The Syrian forces also took Gath in Philistia and, as we have seen, were deterred from invading Judah itself only by the payment of an enormous tribute. Syria was at the height of its power but Israel had reached its lowest ebb.

Jehoash 801-786

The situation now changed. In 805 the Assyrians under Adad-nirari III attacked and crippled Syria. When Jehoash came to the throne, the pressure from Syria was relieved and Israel entered upon a period of growing prosperity.

The main part of the Bible account of his reign consists of the story of the death of Elisha (II Kings 13 *14-21*). Jehoash visited Elisha and used the same words to him as Elisha had used to Elijah, 'the chariots of Israel and the horsemen thereof'. Elisha, too, had been of greater value than military might. Elisha commanded the king to shoot an arrow towards Transjordan* as a symbol and pledge that the territory would be recovered. The fact that afterwards Jehoash only struck the ground three times would be an indication that victory would be limited. Jehoash won three victories over Syria and is said to have recovered all the cities lost by his father. Hazael had died and had been succeeded by his son, Benhadad. There is also here a story of a battle with Judah which Israel won, but we shall look at this story later when we are considering Judah.

Jeroboam II 782-743

The last king of the dynasty of Jehu was Jeroboam II. Despite the fact that his reign occupies only seven verses in the Bible account, he was one of the great military figures of Israel's history. During his reign, Israel reached unparalleled prosperity and gained an empire almost as large as that of Solomon. Assyria was weak and had completely lost control in the west. Jeroboam completed the deliverance from Syria and much territory was annexed. If we are to accept the Biblical account, Jeroboam's territory extended from Hamath, a city far north of Damascus, to the Dead Sea. He developed trade with the Phoenicians and others and this brought Israel into a period of sudden and unexpected prosperity.

Excavations at Megiddo* and Samaria have revealed

something of the prosperity, luxury and height of culture attained during this king's reign. The books of *Amos* and *Hosea* also give a very clear picture of conditions. The Phoenicians were developing their trade and commerce to a great extent. Their ships were sailing to the ends of the earth and Israel shared in the growing prosperity. Add to this the fact that Jeroboam controlled all the main trade routes, and we can understand the reason for the affluence.

But there was a much darker side to all this. The sudden wealth had created a social pyramid. There were shocking contrasts between wealth and poverty. The small farmer was at the mercy of the money-lender and rich landlord. At any misfortune – drought, crop failure or illness – he was liable to be driven out, lose his land and become a slave. We get a picture of these conditions from the book of *Amos*. The wealthy took advantage of the plight of the poor to increase their holdings. Weights and measures were falsified and legal trickery was indulged in (Amos 2 *6*; 5 *11*; 8 *4-6*). The judges could be bribed so that for the poor man there was no hope of justice.

Religion was outwardly flourishing but decadent in quality. The shrines were crowded with eager worshippers and lavishly supported with money (Amos 4 *4*; 5 *21-24*), but the pure religion of Jahveh no longer existed. Many local shrines were openly pagan. The fertility cult was practised everywhere. Many people gave their children names compounded with the name of Baal. The priests and prophetic orders had become time-servers and made no rebuke. At the same time a mood of optimism prevailed. There were no threats from hostile neighbours. The promises of Jahveh were quoted. They looked forward to the coming of a 'Day of the Lord'*, when God would intervene and destroy all their enemies. They claimed the promises of the Covenant but ignored its obligations.

Summary	842-743 BC

Jehu
    a. Purge has left Israel without leaders and without allies.

    b. Jehu pays tribute to Assyria.

    c. Hazael takes the area east of Jordan.

    d. Cult of Baal abolished.

    e. Pagan practices and social injustices allowed to continue.

Jehoahaz
    Vassal to Syria.

Jehoash
    a. Syria crippled by Assyria.

    b. Death of Elisha.

    c. Three victories over Syria.

    d. Battle with Judah.

Jeroboam II
    a. Prosperity due to Assyrian weakness.

    b. Deliverance from Syria complete.

    c. Development of trade.

    d. Luxury, poverty and injustice.

    e. Religion popular but decadent.

    f. Optimistic view of the 'Day of the Lord'.

Questions

1. Tell the story of the visit of Jehoash to Elisha.

2. How do you account for the fact that half the period of Jehu's dynasty was spent in adversity and half in prosperity?

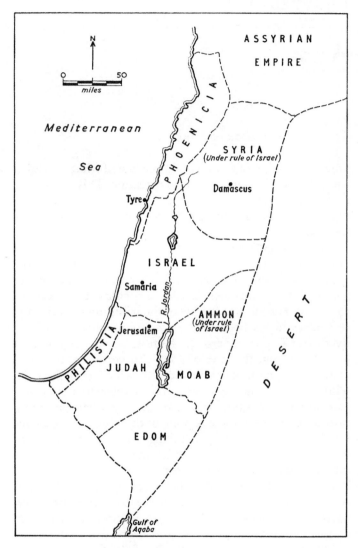

Palestine in the time of Jeroboam II

CHAPTER 10

Amos

To study: The Book of Amos

During the reign of Jeroboam II the first of what are called the 'Writing Prophets' came on the scene. This was Amos, and his message is contained in the book which bears his name. It contains only nine chapters and you should read them all.

Amos prophesied in the Northern kingdom of Israel about 750 BC. He himself was a southerner, coming from the village of Tekoa, about six miles south of Jerusalem in Judah. He was a shepherd who also cultivated a kind of desert fig. His life was the life of the wilderness. Notice the references in his book to the conditions under which he lived. In Chapter 3, verse *12*, he talks about rescuing part of a sheep from the jaws of a lion; in verse *4* of the same chapter he again refers to the lion which inhabited the wilderness. In Chapter 5, verse *19*, he refers to a man running away from a lion only to be met by a bear; or going into a rough desert house and unthinkingly putting his hand against the wall and finding a serpent there. Amos was brought up and lived under the lonely and dangerous conditions of the wilderness.

He probably travelled to Bethel to market his figs and wool. He was very disturbed by the conditions he found there. There was formal worship without reality. The people claimed the promises and protection of God but made no response to the demands of the Covenant. Luxury and poverty went side by side. Notice how Amos describes the conditions of the time in the following passages:

3 *15* refers to the luxurious houses of the rich.

4 *1-3* is a bitter attack upon the women whom he refers to as 'cows of Bashan'. It is they who encourage their husbands to oppress the poor so that they can have their expensive pleasures.

6 *4-6*. Note the picture of luxury here as people recline on the couches listening to the music of the violins, drinking and anointing themselves with perfume, with no thought of the true destiny of the nation.

Alongside all this luxury went injustice.

3 *10* refers to the robbery and violence used to obtain wealth.

8 *4-6*. Note the picture here too. The people are so eager to make money that they cannot wait for the sabbath to be over, and the festivals make them impatient because no profit is being made. They also falsify the balances. 'Ephah' is a weight; 'shekel' is a coin – the point is that people give short weight and charge big prices.

2 *6-8* shows the poor being victimised and the low standards of sexual morality. Compare also 5 *11*.

As Amos tended his sheep and figs alone in the wilderness, he had plenty of time to think. He brooded upon what he had seen and he felt that God was calling him to speak out His Word. Accordingly, the next time he went to Bethel, he drew attention to himself by chanting a dirge, and as the crowd gathered round him he began to speak to them.

At first he denounced the surrounding nations for their wickedness and the crowd applauded. Then he denounced

Judah and at last Israel. He even attacked the king. Amaziah the priest demanded that he should cease and scornfully told him to go back to his own country and prophesy there. Amos denied that he was a prophet, claiming only to be a keeper of sheep whom God had called. Then he disappears from the scene and we hear no more of him. His words were written down and they contain teaching which is important for all time.

The Book of Amos
You should now read the book of *Amos* itself. The following outline will help you. It falls naturally into three sections.

1. Chapters 1 and 2. This is a series of 'doom songs'. Amos condemns Syria (1 *3-5*), Philistia (1 *6-8*), Phoenicia (1 *9-10*), Edom (1 *11-12*) and Ammon (1 *13-15*). He then goes on to denounce Moab (2 *1-3*), Judah (2 *4-5*) and Israel (2 *6-16*).

2. Chapters 3 to 6. Here are three discourses against Israel, each beginning with the phrase 'Hear ye this word.'
   Chapter 3. Inevitable destruction is coming. Because Israel has had so many privileges, she will be punished the more.
   Chapter 4. Amos reproves Israel for oppression, idolatry and their refusal to repent.
   Chapters 5 and 6. He denounces the oppression of the poor (5 *1-17*), formal worship (5 *18-27*) and luxury and excess of all kinds (6).

3. Chapters 7 to 9. A series of visions.
   Chapter 7 *1-6*. A plague of locusts and fire is averted by the prayer of Amos.
   7-9. Amos sees a plumb-line placed against the nation in judgment.
   10-17. This is the only piece of narrative in the book and describes the meeting between Amaziah the priest and Amos.

Chapter 8. Amos sees a basket of summer fruit which looks very beautiful on the outside but is rotten. This suggests to Amos the end of the nation. There is a pun here in the Hebrew language. The Hebrew word for fruits is 'kaits' and for end is 'kets'.

Chapter 9 *1-10*. A vision of Jahveh standing by the altar at Bethel with the command to 'Smite'. It is hopeless to try to escape from His judgment.

11-15. A promise of restoration and glory. Most scholars think this was added by a later writer.

The Message of Amos

You should grasp fully the message of Amos and be able to illustrate it from the book. Pay particular attention to the references given below. His message can be summed up as follows:

1. The greatness and majesty of God. See 4 *13* and 5 *8*. The God whom Amos has met in the desert is the God of the stars and creation.

2. God is the God of all nations. He is concerned about other nations besides Israel. You can see this from the way in which Amos pronounces judgment upon the surrounding nations in Chapters 1 and 2.

3. God is a righteous* God who demands righteousness from His people. See especially Chapter 5 *21-24*. It would be a good thing to learn this passage by heart. Here Amos links morality with religion, a very important step forward.

4. Israel was indeed chosen by God but she was not chosen only for privilege, but also for responsibility. See Chapter 3.

5. Judgment is certain. The 'Day of the Lord'* to which people look forward will surely come, but it will be a day of darkness rather than light. They will not be saved just because they are Israelites. If they do not repent, they will be judged and punished.

Summary	*c.* 760-746 BC

Life of **Amos**	*a.* About 750 BC in reign of Jeroboam II.
	b. Sheep and figs at Tekoa.
	c. Comes to Bethel – meeting with Amaziah.
Message of Amos	*a.* The greatness and majesty of God.
	b. The God of all nations.
	c. The God of righteousness and social justice.
	d. The meaning of Israel's election.
	e. The Day of the Lord will mean judgment for Israel.

Questions

1. Write an account of the meeting between Amos and Amaziah, the priest of Bethel. What was said by the one to the other? What did each mean by what he said?

2. What information does the book of *Amos* give about the life of this prophet? What does Amos say about (*a*) the religion of his contemporaries, and (*b*) their behaviour towards their fellow Israelites?

CHAPTER 11

The Fall of Israel

To study: II Kings 15 and 17

Jeroboam II died in 746. Israel collapsed very quickly after this. A series of kings reigning for very brief periods sets the pattern and all but one of them met death with violence.

At the close of Jeroboam's reign Assyria was beginning to bestir herself. Tiglath-Pileser III (referred to in the Bible by his other name of Pul) seized the Assyrian throne in 745. He conquered Babylon and then turned his eyes to the west. He saw Palestine as a possible base for an attack upon Egypt. Egypt was quick to see the danger and tried to attach the smaller kingdoms to herself, thus forming a series of buffer-states between herself and the great enemy. Most of the history of Israel was then dictated by the conflict between Assyria and Egypt. In Israel there were some who said that alliance with Egypt was the only defence against Assyria. Others said that there could be no defence against Assyria anyway and the best thing to do was to rely upon her protection and make terms with her. These two parties were constantly against each other and the changes on the throne of Israel were largely the result of one party or the other gaining the upper hand. You should also note that Tiglath-Pileser III was the Assyrian monarch who introduced a new policy – that of uprooting conquered peoples. He believed that if the best of a country's leaders were taken away into exile it would kill the national spirit more than anything else. A beaten country could rise again but when a country had lost the best of its population, its character as a nation was gone.

It is against this background then that we watch the later history of Israel. Zachariah, the son of Jeroboam, reigned only six months before he was assassinated (II Kings 15 *8-12*). He was thus the last king of the dynasty of Jehu. His assassin, Shallum, reigned only a few weeks before he in turn was assassinated by Menahem (II Kings 15 *13-15*). Thus we have in one year four kings, two of whom met violent deaths. Menahem was noted for his extreme cruelty (II Kings 15 *16*). He reigned for ten years but the only event reported is that he recognised Assyria as Israel's overlord and paid heavy tribute.

The son of Menahem was Pekahiah who reigned for two years (II Kings 15 *23-26*). He had followed his father's policy of paying tribute to Assyria. Many of the people, including some of the army, were discontented at the continued demands of Assyria and favoured armed resistance. Pekahiah was assassinated by Pekah, an officer in his army.

The next king was the assassin Pekah* (II Kings 15 *27-31*). The Bible says that he reigned for twenty years but this must be wrong. Scholars estimate something between two and five years. He followed a pro-Egyptian policy. During his reign he formed an alliance with Syria and tried to persuade Judah to join this alliance against Assyria. We shall look at this story again when we come to study the history of Judah. It is sufficient to say here that the king of Judah refused to join them and when they attacked him in the hope of putting a more accommodating king on the throne of Judah, the king of Judah appealed to Assyria for help. Assyria moved quickly. Her army came down the coast to take the plain of Philistia to stop any Egyptian intervention. Then she took away from Israel all Galilee and Transjordan* and laid waste Damascus. The whole territory was organised as an Assyrian province and Israel was left as little more than a city-state around

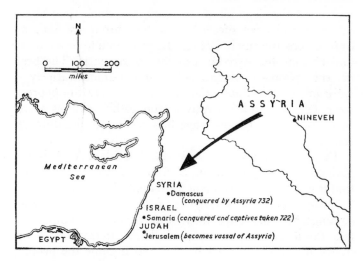

The victory of Assyria

the capital, Samaria. It was only because Pekah had been assassinated in his turn by Hoshea (II Kings 17 *1-6*), who returned to a pro-Assyrian policy and paid tribute, that Israel was left as much territory as that.

Egypt was constantly pressing, however, and had great ambitions of her own. She was not content to see Assyria take control of the world. The problem before Israel and Judah at this time was whether to link themselves more closely with one of the great powers or to keep quietly to themselves and trust in God. The latter was the line of action which the prophets favoured.

In the meantime, Tiglath-Pileser III had been succeeded by Shalmaneser V. With a new king on the throne of Assyria, Hoshea saw his opportunity to rebel and he refused to pay tribute as Pekah had done before him. It was a foolhardy step. Egypt could never save him from Assyria's wrath. Shalmaneser V started the seige of Samaria. It says a good deal for the position and defences of the city that it

69

withstood the siege for three years, by which time Shalmaneser had been succeeded on the throne by Sargon. Sargon took the city in 722 and Israel ceased to be a nation and became the Assyrian province of Samaria. The best of the people – educationally and administratively – were taken away into exile in Assyria. Only the poorest were left, and other captives from other nations were brought in to settle in what had been the kingdom of Israel.

Two other points must be noted. The fall of Israel is explained by the historian in *II Kings* 17 *7-23*. He states that it was a just punishment for Israel's disloyalty to God.

Notice especially *II Kings* 17 *24-28*. This tells about the coming of the foreigners from other parts of the empire to take the place of those deported. They intermarried with the people who were left behind and became the people known as the Samaritans.

Summary   746-722 BC

Tiglath-Pileser of Assyria marches west.

Shall Israel submit or form an alliance with Egypt?

Zechariah

Shallum

Menahem pays tribute to Assyria.

Pekahiah

Pekah   *a.* Supports Egypt.

b. Organises alliance against Assyria which Judah refuses to join.

c. Assyria attacks and subdues Israel.

Hoshea *a.* Supports Assyria.

b. Rebels when Shalmaneser V becomes king of Assyria.

c. Assyria attacks.

d. Samaria falls to Sargon in 722.

e. Deportation.

Questions

1. The policy of Israel was dictated by her position between the great powers. Discuss this.

2. Write notes on:—Tiglath-Pileser III; Menahem; Pekah; Hoshea.

CHAPTER 12

Hosea

To study: Hosea 1, 2, 6 and 11

Before we leave Israel, we must take a brief look at another of her prophets. Hosea prophesied about twenty years after Amos, that is, in the last part of Jeroboam's reign and the confusion which followed. His earliest prophecy was probably in the year of Jeroboam's death. His book is a collection of oracles given at different times. It is not an easy book to read and there is much repetition. If you read the chapters suggested above and look up the other references in this chapter you will have a good idea of his message and importance.

Hosea was a native of Israel and thus felt her sins and failings much more personally than Amos had done. His personal life was a tragedy. He married a girl named Gomer who gave him three children. Hosea named them with symbolic names to suggest God's dealings with Israel. The first was called Jezreel, as a sign of punishment to come; the second 'Not-pitied' to indicate that Jahveh had lost his patience with his people; the third 'Not-my-people' to show that the Covenant* bond had been dissolved.

After a happy period Gomer left Hosea and went after other lovers. At first he was angry (2 2-4), but later found that he loved her so much that he was ready to forgive. He sought her out and found her sold into slavery. He went to her in her shame and bought her back at the price of a slave and after a period of discipline took her back as his wife. He saw that he had a love for her that could not be defeated and he could not let her go.

The important thing is to realise what Hosea made of

this personal situation. *Hosea* 1 *1* and *2* suggests that God commanded him to take a harlot as a wife. What Hosea means is that he saw the hand of God in his experiences. God's will was working through his own life. If he loved her so much that he could not let his wife go, however much she betrayed him, God must love his people even more. Hosea takes his own experience and sees in it a parable of God's relationship to Israel.

Jahveh had chosen Israel. The Exodus was the sign of his choosing. He had called Israel out of Egypt (11 *1*). The Covenant* was Jahveh's marriage to His people. But Israel had broken the Covenant. All her troubles were but symptoms of the disease of faithlessness. The two great themes of Hosea are the utter sinfulness of Israel (she is a 'deceitful bow' and commits 'great whoredoms') and the faithful love of Jahveh.

Hosea puts down all the evils around him as being due to a corrupt religion. He therefore condemns the priests (4 *4-6*). He attacks the idolatry which has crept in and the licentious practices which always accompanied idolatry. (Note Chapter 10 and the references to the local 'Baals' in 2 *8* and *13*). Look up also in this connection 4 *17*, 8 *5* and 13 *2*. The result of faithlessness is that Israel has become a 'cake not turned' (7 *8*). There is no balance, no harmony. There are glaring contrasts of wealth and poverty.

Through all this faithlessness, however, the Love of God remains constant. Jahveh wishes to heal His people (7 *1*) and to redeem them as Hosea redeemed his wife (7 *13*). Read and make your own summary of Chapter 11. In this chapter the first four verses speak of the Love of God; verses *5* to *7* show how God's patience is exhausted; verses *8* to *9* speak of judgment but show that judgment is not God's final word.

Hosea's warning fell on deaf ears. The situation was therefore hopeless. They had 'sowed the wind' and therefore would 'reap the whirlwind' (8 *7*). A judgment is coming from which there is no escape. We can sum up the message of Hosea as follows:

1. God's love for His people is never quenched and even when He has to punish them it is His way of bringing them back to Him.

2. God is spiritual and holy and demands from His people not sacrifices, but obedience and mercy. Note especially in this connection Chapter 6 verse 6. Remember that in this verse 'knowledge of God' is not intellectual knowledge but rather a right relationship with Him. The Hebrew word 'to know' referred to the closest possible relationship.

3. Punishment and suffering will surely come but the suffering can be a discipline to lead men back to God.

Summary   *c*. 750-730 BC

Hosea   *a*. About twenty years after Amos in the period of confusion.

b. Native of Israel.

c. His personal life gives him the key to Jahveh's relations with Israel.

d. Israel's ill-fortune the result of a corrupt religion.

Message *a*. Sinfulness of Israel and faithful love of Jahveh.

b. Condemns idolatry and social injustice.

c. The love of God remains constant.

d. God demands obedience and mercy.

e. Punishment will come but can be a discipline.

Question

Compare Amos and Hosea. In what ways are they alike and in what ways do they differ as prophets of God?

Summary of the Relations between Israel and Syria   922-722 BC

Benhadad I attacks Baasha at the request of Asa, king of Judah. *I Kings* 15.

Omri gives up territory east of Jordan. *I Kings* 20 *34*.

Ahab's war with Syria. *I Kings* 20.

Ahab attacks Ramoth-Gilead. *I Kings* 22.

Border warfare in Jehoram's reign. The story of Naaman. *II Kings* 5.

Syrian attack on Israel. *II Kings* 6.

Hazael anointed king of Syria by Elisha. *II Kings* 8.

Jehoram and Ahaziah of Judah, fighting at Ramoth-Gilead (Jehu). *II Kings* 8.

Hazael attacks Jehu who places himself under the protection of Shalmaneser. Later, Hazael takes all the land east of Jordan from Israel.

Jehoahaz a vassal of Hazael. *II Kings* 13.

Alliance between Syria and Israel to attack Judah in the reign of Pekah of Israel.

Summary of the Relations between Israel and Judah   922-722 BC

Constant warfare in the reign of Rehoboam.

Abijah defeats Jeroboam I. *II Chronicles* 13.

Baasha attacks Asa of Judah who appeals to Syria. *I Kings* 15.

Marriage between Athaliah and Jehoram. *II Kings* 8 *18*.

Jehoshaphat joins with Ahab to attack Ramoth-Gilead. *I Kings* 22.

Jehoram of Israel and Ahaziah of Judah at Ramoth-Gilead (Jehu). *II Kings* 9.

Israel and Syria attack Judah in reign of Pekah of Israel.

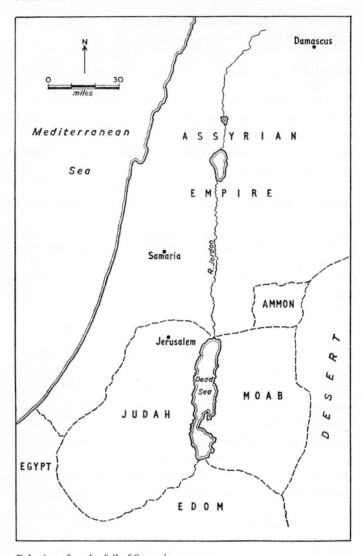

Palestine after the fall of Samaria, 722 BC

CHAPTER 13

The Decline of Judah

To study: II Kings 14, 15 *32-38*, 16
             Compare II Chronicles 26

After the assassination of Joash, king of Judah, Amaziah (800-783) came to the throne. On the whole he seems to have been a good king. He put to death his father's murderers but would not kill their children. He succeeded in conquering Edom and taking her capital, Sela. This was an important step. So long as Edom was independent and unfriendly she could block Judah's route to the Red sea. Solomon's wealth had depended upon this route being open. Amaziah succeeded in reopening the trade route and thus increased Judah's prosperity.

The expedition to Edom had, however, an unfortunate sequel. Amaziah, confident in his strength, foolishly challenged Israel. The reason for the challenge is given in *II Chronicles* 25 *5-24*. Amaziah had hired Israelite help to supplement his own forces against Edom. Deciding not to use them after all, he sent them home. They expressed their anger at this insult by looting a number of Judean towns on their way home. When Amaziah heard of this on his return he declared war on Israel. The reply of Jehoash is given in *II Kings* 14 *9-10*. He compared himself to a cedar and Amaziah to a little thistle liable to be crushed by any passing beast. He told Amaziah to be content with what he had won. Amaziah, however, persisted in his challenge with the result that he was utterly defeated, Jerusalem was despoiled and the temple robbed.

A conspiracy against Amaziah forced him to flee from his capital. He was probably hoping to find refuge in Egypt but his enemies caught him at Lachish, 35 miles south-west of Jerusalem, and he was assassinated.

He was succeeded by Uzziah (sometimes called Azariah) (783-742). Uzziah had a long and prosperous reign. At this time Judah shared something of the prosperity which was being enjoyed by Israel under Jeroboam II. The record of his reign in the Bible is very meagre. The eight verses in *II Kings* 15 are supplemented by an account in *II Chronicles* 26. From these we learn that he had successful campaigns against the Philistines and the Arabs and exacted tribute from the Ammonites. He rebuilt the port of Elath, formerly called Ezion-Geber, on the Gulf of Aqaba. He was credited with repairing the defences of Jerusalem, reorganising the army and developing agriculture. Unfortunately he caught leprosy. The Chronicler says that it was because in his pride he tried to take over the priestly function of offering incense. During the latter part of his reign Jotham, his son, acted as Regent.

When Uzziah died, Jotham succeeded to the throne (742-735) but we know nothing of his reign except that he built a new gate to the Temple.

His successor was Ahaz (735-715) and about him the writer of *Kings* has nothing good to say. He revived some of the pagan practices of the ancient religion, allowed wizards and those with familiar spirits and even indulged in human sacrifice. The great event of his reign was the Syro-Ephraimite war.

We have already spoken of the pressure being exerted by Assyria under Tiglath-Pileser III. In one of his inscriptions Tiglath-Pileser says that in his early campaigns against Syria he was confronted by a large western coalition of forces headed by Uzziah of Judah. In fact, according to Assyrian inscriptions, Uzziah must have been one of the strongest political forces in the west. At any rate it seems

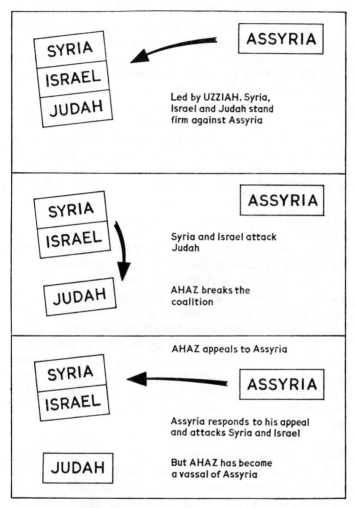

The Syro-Ephraimite War

According to Tiglath Pileser III, Uzziah of Judah led a coalition against him

79

as though he led a coalition of Judah, Israel and Syria in order to stand against the might of Assyria. When Uzziah died the coalition lost its leader. We are not certain exactly what happened. There was possibly another attempt to form the coalition in which Ahaz refused to join. It may be that the coalition was still in existence and Ahaz deliberately withdrew. However it happened, Syria and Israel wanted a combination of forces against Assyria, and Ahaz refused. Pekah*, king of Israel, and Rezin*, king of Syria, joined forces to attack Ahaz. They aimed to remove him and to place someone on the throne who would be more willing to join in with their plans. Edom also rebelled at this time and the Philistines attacked, so that Judah was being attacked on three sides. Ahaz appealed to Assyria for help. We have already seen the result. Assyria attacked and subdued Syria and Israel. But Ahaz had to pay the price for Assyria's assistance. He had to go to Damascus to pay homage to the king of Assyria. He had to become a vassal and pay a heavy tribute for 'protection'. In addition he was required to set up a special altar in the Temple precincts. This was quite a common thing for a vassal nation to be asked to do. By setting up an altar to the gods of the conquerors a kingdom acknowledged vassalship and alliance. An altar to a foreign deity in the Temple at Jerusalem, however, was unthinkable and Ahaz was regarded as having brought his country as low as she could possibly go.

The end of Ahaz's reign saw Judah as a satellite nation, so different from the kingdom of Uzziah. Foreign territory had been lost and heavy tribute had to be paid to Assyria. The loss of territory meant loss of revenue and yet more demands were made by the conquerors. The great landlords dispossessed the poor. The judges and priests were corrupt and Judah had declined.

Summary 800-715 BC

Amaziah *a.* Re-opens the route to the sea by conquest of Edom.

b. Foolishly challenges Israel and is humiliated.

Uzziah *a.* A reign of prosperity.

b. Successful military campaigns.

c. Repairs defences of Jerusalem and reorganises army.

d. Leprosy.

Jotham

Ahaz *a.* Revives many pagan practices.

b. Syro-Ephraimite war.

c. Becomes vassal of Assyria.

d. Judah as a satellite nation.

Question

Write what you know about the causes and consequences of the Syro-Ephraimite war.

The Chart to the Fall of Samaria

Egypt	Judah	Israel	Syria	Mesopotamia
900 BC	*Rehoboam*	*Jeroboam I*		
Shishak —→				
	Abijah			
	Asa	Nadab		
	←	—Baasha ←	—*Benhadad I*	
		Elah		
		Zimri		
	Jehoshaphat	*Omri*		*Shalmaneser III*
850 BC		*Ahab* ———	→ Ramoth-Gilead	(Battle of Qarqar)
		Elijah		
		Ahaziah		
		Elisha		
	Jehoram	*Jehoram*		
	Ahaziah	*Jehu*		
	Athaliah			
	Joash ←———		—Hazael	
		Jehoahaz		
800 BC	Amaziah	*Jehoash* ———	→ Benhadad ←	—Adad-nirari III
		Jeroboam II		
750 BC	Uzziah	**Amos**		
		Zachariah		Tiglath Pileser III
		Hosea		
		Shallum		
	Jotham	*Menahem*	Rezin	
		Pekahiah	←——	
	Ahaz ←———	—Pekah	Fall of Damascus 732	
		Isaiah		
		Hoshea		Shalmaneser V
		Fall of Samaria ← 722	——	—Sargon

CHAPTER 14

The Prophet Isaiah

To study: Isaiah 1 to 8

During the reign of Ahaz we get the first word from the prophet Isaiah, one of the greatest prophets of the Old Testament. Unlike the earlier prophets, he was a man of the city. He may have been of the blood royal and he was certainly a courtier and a member of the privileged circles in Jerusalem. He did not look back to the wilderness and the early Covenant days like Amos and Hosea. He was concerned more to speak of the relationship between the dynasty of David and Jahveh. He assembled a body of disciples around him and became the leader of a religious movement.

His work was mainly centred around three crises in his nation's life.

1. The first was the Syro-Ephraimite war when Ahaz, frightened of Syria and Israel, asked for help from Assyria.

2. During the reign of Hezekiah, who succeeded Ahaz, a party was formed to break with Assyria and form an alliance with Egypt. Isaiah was strongly opposed to this and his policy prevailed.

3. During the time of Sennacherib, king of Assyria, there was a general revolt of the vassal states. Judah was drawn in despite the protests of Isaiah. However, when Sennacherib attacked, Isaiah told the king that Jerusalem would not fall and he was proved right.

In this chapter we shall study Isaiah's general message

and his message in the reign of Ahaz. We shall deal with the later crises when we come to the reign of Hezekiah.

You should read *Isaiah* 6 first because this chapter describes his call to be a prophet. During the reign of Uzziah, Isaiah had been happy at the court. Everything seemed to be going well before the blow fell. Uzziah died in a leper house. The young king was anything but strong in character. The might of Assyria was ominous in the east. Isaiah, bowed down by events, went into the house of God. There he saw *the* king upon whom all destinies finally depend. Above him stood the seraphim – literally 'burning ones' – heavenly beings giving added sense to the holiness of the experience. Each one, we are told, had six wings – two covered his face in reverence, two covered his feet in humility and with two he was ready to fly to do the bidding of God. Isaiah had a sense of the sheer holiness of God – a theme which was to dominate all his preaching through the years. God's holiness made Isaiah realise his own uncleanness – in the presence of the Creator nothing unclean can survive. The prophet himself had to be purified before he could speak. Then, purified, he heard the call of God and responded. He was told that people would not listen to him. His work was to be in some senses a failure but there would be a remnant with whom God could begin anew.

The main theme of this chapter can be summed up as: Vision of the Perfect – sense of unworthiness – cleansing – willingness for service. The earlier chapters elaborate this theme.

Now read the other chapters set for study with the help of the following notes:

Chapter 1

Isaiah's message is set out here in the form of a trial at law. The Judge and the plaintiff are God. The assessors or jury are heaven and earth. Judah is the defendant and the prophet is the witness.

2 and *3*. Heaven and earth are called to witness the infidelity and ingratitude of Judah.

4-9. A lament over the calamity and desolation which have fallen upon the land. The sin of Judah is the primary cause.

10-17. A denunciation of sacrifice as practised in Judah.

18-20. An appeal and a warning.

21-28. An elegy over sinful Jerusalem.

29-31. Two fragments – notice the condemnation of tree worship. A main feature of this chapter is that God reasons with men. True religion is something which is rational and moral – reasonable intercourse between one intelligent being and another. Against this is the unworthy religion of smoky sacrifice and ritual. They pray but do not think. God will not let them alone; He compels them to think.

We see here God in two aspects – the infinitely high and the infinitely near. Notice also the love of God, 'I have nourished children' – these are the words of a father. The message is followed by a demand that religion must be applied to everyday life and relationships.

Chapters 2 to 4

These chapters contain a picture of three cities.

2 *2-5*. This is the ideal city – a kind of Utopia. This passage is also found in *Micah* 4 *1-4*. It may be anonymous and adapted by both prophets to put at the head of their message.

2 *6* to 4 *1*. The actual city. Nothing is worth preserving. Note the sarcasm in 3 *6* and the attack on the women in 3 *16* to 4 *2*.

4 *2-6*. The city as she shall be. This is the ideal and there will be no need for punishment.

Chapter 5. The Song of the Vineyard.

The song is contained in verses *1* to *7* and is fairly straightforward. What more could the owner have done? Yet instead of grapes there were only wild grapes. The only thing to do now is to abandon the vineyard. The meaning is obvious, for Israel was often spoken of as the vineyard of God. Jahveh will abandon her to her foes. The rest of the chapter contains what is almost a catalogue of the 'wild grapes' and this part of the chapter illustrates the social message of the prophet.

8-10 refer to the landgrabbers and contain a denunciation of land monopoly.

11-17. An attack upon luxury and drink and irresponsible wealth.

18-21. The people are guilty of moral blindness. They confuse moral issues and at the same time are overwhelmed with conceit.

22-24 return to the condemnation of drink and money.

25-30. God's judgment is coming. Verse *25* speaks of the anger of God and *26-30* describe a coming invader who will execute Jahveh's righteous judgment on His people. Chapters 7 and 8 deal with the Syro-Ephraimite war.

Chapter 7

Ahaz is in a 'tight spot' (verse *2*, 'moved like the trees by the wind') – and is afraid. He goes to inspect the water supply in preparation for a siege. Isaiah takes his son (Shear-jashub – meaning 'a remnant shall return'[1]) and meets him. His message is 'Trust in Jahveh and keep calm.' In verse *4* he tells Ahaz that his two enemies are only 'smoking firebrands' almost burnt out. They are men, not God. All Ahaz needs is complete commitment to God.

When Ahaz does not believe, Isaiah tells him to ask for a sign. He declines under the pretence of piety, but really because he has already made up his mind what he is going to do.

Isaiah is exasperated – Jahveh will give a sign. A girl

[1] See note at end of this chapter.

will give birth to a baby and call his name 'Emmanuel'. Before he reaches the age when he knows right from wrong the alliance will be broken and Syria and Ephraim will be defeated but punishment will still come upon Judah.

In verses *18-25* Jahveh summons Egypt and Assyria to exact his vengeance. Notice the symbols of 'fly' and 'bee' for Egypt and Assyria and the fine irony behind 'he shall shave with an Assyrian razor'.

Chapter 8
This begins with a renewed warning. Isaiah's second son is born and called 'Speed the spoil, haste the prey'. Before the child will be able to say 'Daddy' and 'Mummy' the Assyrian king will plunder Damascus and Samaria. Isaiah writes the same message on a tablet to bear witness. Verses *5* and *6* describe the rejection of the waters of Shiloah, a little aqueduct into the city, for the rivers of Assyria. The gentle stream is a symbol of quiet faith in Jahveh. Isaiah was met by the stubborn resistance of a faithless generation. His message fell upon deaf ears.

At this stage Isaiah withdrew into the prophetic circle with his followers (8 *11–16*). This was to be the 'remnant' with a different allegiance. They would trust and wait. This was to be the nucleus of the new Israel and the message was sealed for a future day when it would be understood and accepted.

Isaiah delivered a message which in some ways is reminiscent of Amos. He denounced the nobles and the judges who could be bribed and the decadent upper classes. Over all his thinking and speaking is the sense of the awful holiness of God. He never forgot the vision which first called him to be a prophet. He realised from the beginning that he was speaking to people who were incapable of correction. The message in the Temple had prepared him for the rejection of his message. The only alternative to accepting his message was judgment. The Day of Jahveh would be therefore a Day of Judgment. Assyria would be the instrument of God to punish His people.

On the other hand, he had been promised that a 'stump' would remain and this was his great hope. It is with Isaiah that the doctrine of the remnant comes to the fore. There are indications of this principle – that God will save by the few – earlier in the story. We remember the seven thousand who had not bowed to Baal in the Elijah story. Isaiah concentrated on this. If only a remnant will accept the message, the remnant *will* be saved and *will* be faithful. There is the hope for the future.

NOTE ON SHEAR-JASHUB

It was a custom for people to give their children symbolic names. For example, many people gave their children names compounded with the name of 'Jahveh' such as Jehoash, Jehoram. Others used the name of Baal in a similar way, e.g. Jerubbaal, Ishbaal.

We have seen that Hosea gave his children symbolic names to emphasise his message. Isaiah's first son is therefore called 'Shear-jashub' which means a 'remnant shall return'. This means simply 'a remnant shall repent'. When we remember Isaiah's call we can see that this means that only a remnant of the people shall be saved and from that point of view it is a solemn warning. On the other hand there is a more hopeful meaning too. However much the people turn away from God a remnant *shall* repent and with that remnant God will accomplish His purposes. This is one of the basic messages of Isaiah – the doctrine of the remnant. The name of his son sums up therefore a vital part of his message.

Summary   *c.* 740-670 BC

Isaiah *a.* A man of the city and the court.

       b. The prophet as politician at three great crises.

His message

       a. The Holiness of God (6).

       b. God's complaint against Judah (1).

       c. The three cities (2 to 4).

       d. The Song of the Vineyard (5).

       e. The Syro-Ephraimite war (7, 8):

          i. Trust in Jahveh;
          ii. The Sign of Emmanuel.

       f. The remnant.

Questions

1. Write out the substance of Isaiah's parable of the Vineyard. What did the prophet mean to teach by means of this parable?

2. Write an account of the interview between the prophet Isaiah and king Ahaz, making clear in your answer the nature of the problem which then faced the king and the nature and meaning of the sign promised to the king by the prophet.

CHAPTER 15

The Reign of Hezekiah

To study: II Kings 18, 19
II Chronicles 29 to 31
Isaiah 18, 20, 30 *1-7*, 31 *1-3*, 36, 37

Throughout the reign of Ahaz, Judah remained submissive to Assyria. Patriotic people in Judah resented this bitterly. *Hezekiah* (715-687) reversed his father's policy at almost every point. He is one of the two kings for whom the chronicler has only words of praise. He desired purity of worship and freedom for his people. At first cautiously, therefore, and later more boldly he tried to get free from the Assyrian yoke.

The situation in Judah itself was very difficult. Social abuses and tendencies to worship idols which had grown up in the reign of Ahaz continued. The Assyrian altar was still in the temple and this, combined with the cult which surrounded it, was not only offensive to the loyal Jews but a constant reminder of national humiliation. For this position, however, there was no remedy so long as Judah remained a tributary of Assyria. To have abolished the worship of the Assyrian gods would have been deemed an act of rebellion and brought the might of Assyria to the gates of Jerusalem. Assyrian taxes had also to be paid. There was widespread discontent and the profound hope that the new king would restore freedom and pure worship.

The world situation also raised hopes. There was a rebellion in Babylon under a Chaldean prince, Merodach-Baladan, which caused Sargon to lose control in that part

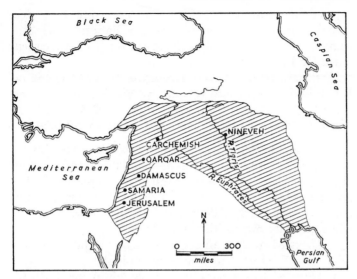

The Empire of Assyria, *c.* 700 BC

of his empire. He had to conduct campaigns in many different places. While he was busily occupied putting down rebellion, Egypt was recovering her strength. A stirring of rebellion was everywhere. Philistia actually did rebel and invited Judah, Edom and Moab to join in a bid for freedom.

Opinions in Judah were divided. Some felt that the time was ripe to throw off the Assyrian yoke; others were hesitant for they knew something of what Assyrian vengeance would mean if the attempt failed. Could Egypt be depended upon to give her promised support? The atmosphere was full of expectancy. Envoys came from Ethiopia to consult with Hezekiah. Isaiah was bitterly opposed to the rebellion. He called upon the king to refuse the envoys from Ethiopia. He illustrated the folly of trusting in Egypt by walking about Jerusalem in a loin-cloth. The message he gave was that just as he was walking about in a loin-cloth and barefooted, so would the Assyrian king lead away

91

captive those who rebelled. The king listened to his advice and took it. Judah did not rebel. The nations which did were crushed by the might of Assyria but Judah escaped harm (Is 18 and 20).

Hezekiah, however, was anxious to reform the life of Judah both socially and religiously. His reforms are very important and you should study them in *II Kings* 18 *3-6* and *II Chronicles* 29 to 31. Here is a summary of them:

1. He set aside the foreign practices of Ahaz. He also removed the various cult objects associated with the worship of Jahveh because they were leading the people into idolatry. He destroyed the brazen serpent (supposedly that made by Moses in the wilderness) and called it Nehushtan*, which literally means 'the brass thing'.

2. He tried to close all the local shrines of Jahveh – the 'high places' which had seen so much idolatry.

3. He tried to persuade the people left in the north to join in rallying round Jerusalem as a centre of worship. His idea was to unite the whole country – what was left of Israel as well as Judah – under the throne of David. This was planned as a prelude to a bid for independence. His invitation received a rebuff in Israel, partly because of jealousy and partly because Assyria had recognised Bethel as a legal sanctuary.

4. He introduced vessels bearing the stamp of the king. This was an attempt to standardise weights and measures in order to prevent dishonesty.

There was no open break with Assyria so long as Sargon was king. When, however, he was succeeded by his son, Sennacherib, the time seemed opportune and Hezekiah refused to pay the tribute. The rebellion broke out again when Merodach-Baladan of Babylon, seizing the opportunity presented by a change of leadership of Assyria, revolted and established himself as king. He sent embassies to all the smaller states inviting them to join him so that

Sennacherib would be faced with rebellion in every part of his empire. Merodach-Baladan was strong and Sennacherib was kept occupied many months before he managed to defeat him.

In the meantime, revolt had also broken out in the west. A coalition was formed with Tyre, Philistia, Moab and Edom, and Judah was invited to join in. Despite the renewed warnings of Isaiah, Hezekiah did join the revolt. He sent envoys to Egypt to ask for help and became one of the leaders in the rebellion. He realised the seriousness of the battle ahead and busied himself seeing to his defences. It was about this time that he built the famous Siloam tunnel which still exists today. The position was that water had to be brought into Jerusalem from the spring of Gihon, outside the city walls, to the Pool of Siloam, inside the walls. In time of siege the water supply could be cut off by an enemy capturing the spring. Hezekiah overcame this difficulty by cutting a tunnel 1,700 feet long through the solid rock from the spring to the pool. Workers using wedges, hammers and picks started at both ends and met in the middle. An inscription on the wall of this tunnel, now in the Istanbul museum, says 'while there was yet three cubits to be bored through, there was heard the voice of one calling to another.' This tunnel was one of the most remarkable engineering feats of ancient times.

Most of the smaller nations joined together in this rebellion but Padi, king of Ekron, refused. His subjects rose against him and took him prisoner and he was taken to Jerusalem for custody. (You can read about this rebellion in *II Kings* 18 *7* and 20 *20*, *II Chronicles* 32 *30*, *Isaiah* 30 and 31.)

In 701 BC Sennacherib had defeated Merodach-Baladan and was ready to turn to the west. He marched through the Fertile Crescent and, turning south, crushed Tyre. When the other small nations saw what was happening they began to break away from the rebellion. Moab and Edom rushed to Sennacherib to pay tribute and thus try to escape his vengeance. Only Ashkelon, Ekron and Judah continued the fight. Sennacherib marched south and defeated Ashkelon and Ekron, wiping out the Egyptian army on the way, and turned against Judah. He reduced forty-six Judean fortified cities and deported their populations. He shut up Hezekiah and his troops in Jerusalem. His own words are very expressive when he says that he shut up Hezekiah 'like a bird in a cage'. The slaughter in Judah was terrible. Excavations at Lachish have unearthed a pit containing the remains of 1,500 bodies covered with debris. The land was devastated.

Hezekiah saw that the rebellion was finished and he sent to Sennacherib to sue for terms. They were very severe terms indeed. Padi, king of Ekron, had to be released. Judah's territory was divided up. The tribute money was greatly increased. Hezekiah had to strip the Temple and the royal treasury to pay it. Other presents had to be given including some of Hezekiah's daughters as concubines (*II Kings* 18).

The story is somewhat confused after this. A straightforward reading of the account in *II Kings* suggests that Sennacherib later considered that this was not enough and he demanded a total surrender of the city. He sent the Rabshakeh* (a title for the chief general) to demand total surrender. Read the story in *II Kings* 18 *17* – 19 *37*. The general called out to the nobles demanding the surrender of the city and saying that no help was going to come from Egypt. He spoke in Hebrew, the language of Jerusalem, and his voice carried into the city. The nobles asked that he should speak in Aramaic, the language of diplomacy, to which he replied that his message was to the people and not the rulers. He was obviously trying to appeal to the common people in the hope that they would force their leaders to open the city gates. But the army remained loyal. Hezekiah preferred to die fighting rather than surrender. The siege continued until the people were on the verge of despair. The king then sent two of his nobles, Eliakim* and Shebnah*, to Isaiah. They were probably the leaders of two parties in Jerusalem – Eliakim preferring to submit to Assyria, and Shebnah leading a group who advocated making an alliance with Egypt. Isaiah assured the king through them that despite appearances, the city would not fall. One of the strangest things in history followed. The Bible tells us that in one night many Assyrian soldiers died and Sennacherib had to return home.

As Byron expressed it,

> 'The might of the Gentile, unsmote by the
>   sword,
> Hath melted like snow in the glance of the Lord.'

What exactly happened is hard to say. The suggestion has been made that a number of mice had brought the bubonic plague amongst Sennacherib's army. Others have suggested that disturbing news had come from Assyria and Sennacherib had to hurry away. All we can say for certain is that this was a most remarkable deliverance.

Isaiah's words were remembered and the belief grew in Judah that Zion would remain inviolate against any conqueror.

Some scholars think, however, that we have here the accounts of two campaigns which have got mixed together. They suggest that after Hezekiah had paid the tribute, Sennacherib went away. Assyrian reverses elsewhere and the coming of a new ruler in Egypt encouraged Hezekiah to rebel a second time. Sennacherib could do nothing immediately for he was occupied elsewhere. When he did turn west again he broke through the forces of Judah and blockaded Hezekiah in Jerusalem a second time. It was on this occasion that he sent his Rabshakeh to demand surrender. As the original coming of Sennacherib was about 701 BC, if there was a second invasion it is thought that it was in 688 BC.

Shortly after this Hezekiah fell ill. Merodach-Baladan, the king of Babylon, sent envoys with a present for him. Hezekiah showed these messengers all the treasures of Jerusalem and he was strongly rebuked by Isaiah for doing so (II Kings 20 *12-19*).

Hezekiah died in the year following Sennacherib's sudden withdrawal from Jerusalem. His son, Manasseh, gave up the rebellion and made peace.

Summary   715-687 BC

Hezekiah *a.* Reversed the policy of Ahaz.

      b. Isaiah warns against revolt and is heeded.

      c. Hezekiah's reforms:

            i. Foreign pagan practices abolished.
            ii. Nehushtan.
            iii. Attempts to abolish 'high places'.
            iv. Tries to unite with the people of the North.
            v. Standardises weights and measures.

      d. On Sennacherib's accession Hezekiah refuses tribute to Assyria.

      e. Revolt against the advice of Isaiah.

      f. Siloam tunnel constructed.

      g. Sennacherib besieges Jerusalem and is bought off.

      h. A possible second invasion and siege. Jerusalem is delivered.

Questions

---

1. What reforms were carried out in the religious life of Judah by king Hezekiah?

2. Describe the scene when the Assyrian general demands the surrender of Jerusalem.

3. Write notes on: – Sennacherib; Merodach-Baladan; Nehushtan.

4. 'Isaiah was a statesman of no mean calibre.' Discuss this statement.

CHAPTER 16

Micah

To study: Micah 1-3, 6 *6-8*

During the time that Sennacherib was invading Judah, another prophet spoke out the word of God. Micah was a countryman whereas Isaiah was a man of the city. He was not so much concerned with international politics as Isaiah but rather with injustice at home.

We know very little about his personal life except that he came from Moresheth-gath, a little village in the hills about 25 miles south-west of Jerusalem. It was in the Shephelah – the famous foot-hill-country of Palestine. It was a very fertile country with vines and olives everywhere, rolling cornfields and sheep grazing on every pasture, a typical farmers' country which should have been happy and prosperous. Micah was a countryman himself and he spoke for the poor farmers who were suffering at the hands of the powerful landlords. The situation was as follows. During the very prosperous reign of Uzziah money had begun to flow very freely. Wealth had added to wealth and created a new capitalist class in Jerusalem. These wealthy men had ambitions to own land and acquire estates. In order to do so they dispossessed the peasant farmers. The method was to offer to lend money on mortgage when farmers were hard-up, as they often were. It was lent on exorbitant interest and when the farmer could not pay the mortgage was foreclosed. The farm was taken over by the man who had given the loan and the farmer had no redress. Gradually, the peasant farmers were pushed out by the money-grabbing class and had to drift to the towns seeking work. Here they either lived in helpless poverty or sold themselves as slaves.

It is interesting to notice as one reads the book of *Micah* how the details of the situation are described. Note especially Chapter 2 *1, 2* and *9* for a picture of land-grabbing and what it meant; 2 *8* gives a picture of the creditors; 6 *10-11* shows the fraudulent trading. The rulers and judges are attacked in 3 *1-3*, because they will not execute justice, and in 3 *5-8* we have an attack on the leaders of religion because they, too, are corrupt. Chapter 7 *2-6* gives a picture of evil everywhere. It is useful to note these and other passages as you read, for you can often build up a picture of the conditions from the actual words of a book.

Micah maintained that the corruption of Israel had come to Judah (1 *8, 9*), but Jahveh was coming to execute judgment (1 *1-9*). He probably had in mind the coming of Assyria as the instrument of Jahveh's judgment. He made a great attack on the cities (note esp. 1 *5*). The original nomads had a great suspicion of cities; the city dweller was often regarded as a sinner. The Rechabites were an extreme illustration of this attitude and many people sympathised with them. Here Micah was expressing the same point of view. He was saying that the sins of Israel and Judah were supremely those of the cities, Samaria and Jerusalem. He contrasted himself with the professional prophets as Amos had done earlier (3 *5-8*). Zion, i.e. Jerusalem, had been built with blood (3 *10*) and would fall into ruins. Here again is a contrast with Isaiah. Isaiah, despite all his prophecies of judgment, maintained that Jerusalem itself would not fall. Micah was quite sure that the city would be destroyed.

The message of Micah can be summed up in a few words. Social corruption would bring forth the deserved punishment from a righteous God. He called for repentance and the repentance he sought was, above all else, social reform.

Micah was a great democrat and he demanded that the service of God should be shown in right dealings with men. All the time he had in mind the men he knew so well – the farmers who were beaten down under injustice and oppression. He was not concerned with international politics. He was too much overwhelmed by the injustice within the nation. Unless it was put right it was bound to bring forth vengeance from God.

In your reading of the book of *Micah* pay particular attention to Chapter 6 verses *6-8*. This sums up not only the message of Micah but the message of all the prophets. It is one of the greatest passages in the Old Testament and you should know it by heart.

Notice also the reference in Chapter 5 verses *1 – 3* about the ruler who is to come out of Bethlehem.

Summary   *c.* 725-701 BC

Micah *a.* Contemporary with Isaiah.

    b. Differences from Isaiah:

        i. Micah a countryman.

        ii. Concerned about injustice at home rather than international politics.

        iii. Micah says Jerusalem will fall.

His message

    a. Primarily against oppression of farmers.

    b. Social injustice will bring forth the vengeance of God.

    c. Attack on cities.

    d. Repentance implies social reform.

    e. The service of God to be expressed in right dealings with men.

Questions

1. Compare and contrast the messages of Isaiah and Micah.

2. Summarise the social conditions existing in Judah in the time of Micah and illustrate from the prophet's teaching.

CHAPTER 17

The Contribution of the Eighth-Century Prophets

We saw how prophecy began in Israel with wandering bands of enthusiasts for Jahveh and how it degenerated into groups of 'false prophets' and time-servers at the court. We saw also how an individual would separate himself, conscious of a call from God, and speak a particular word of God in a particular situation. Such men were Nathan, Ahijah, Micah and above all, Elijah and Elisha.

We saw also how Elijah in his contests with Ahab turned away the people of Israel from polytheism*. They must only worship Jahveh. That did not mean that there were no other gods. Other nations could have other gods and Israel accepted them as real for those nations, but Israel must worship only Jahveh. This belief is called *Monolatry** – a belief in many gods, but only One is to be worshipped.

Despite Elijah, the people often introduced practices from other religions into their worship of Jahveh. Jahveh was worshipped at the high places* of Canaanite religion and it is easy to see how some of the practices of that religion came to be adopted into the worship of Israel's God. This 'mixing' of religions is known as *Syncretism** and it was a constant danger in Israel.

Israel worshipped Jahveh because He had delivered them from Egypt and chosen them at Sinai and made a Covenant. This meant that Jahveh would look after them and in their turn they would be faithful to Jahveh. If they had enemies, Jahveh would defeat those enemies because He was stronger than the gods of those enemies.

The Golden Age of prophecy began in the eighth century BC and lasted for some three hundred years. The prophet now was entirely different from the early prophets who had worked themselves into a frenzy. The chief characteristic which was common to all the great prophets was the consciousness of an individual call. 'Thus saith the Lord' was the prophetic introduction. Each one of them spoke under a strong sense of constraint. It was something he had to do whether he wanted to do it or not. When the people refused his message he put it into writing. In fact, it is doubtful if anything would have been written down at all if the people to whom the word was addressed had accepted it. But the prophet wished to place on record what he had said and if he was not able to do it himself he usually had disciples who would.

The eighth-century prophets took a further step in revealing the truth about God. Amos stated quite clearly that Jahveh was concerned with other nations besides Israel. He prophesied punishment for Edom, Damascus, Moab and other countries – punishment from Israel's God for their various sins. This was an important step which Isaiah was to take even further. When Isaiah looked at the situation in his time he was confronted with a great problem. In Israel's conflicts with her enemies it was always assumed that Jahveh was more powerful than the gods of those enemies and therefore He could deliver her. But Israel was helpless before Assyria. Did this mean that Assyria's gods were more powerful than Jahveh? If it did not mean this it must have meant that Jahveh was also the God of Assyria and was using her for his purposes. This latter view was the view that Isaiah took. He even described Assyria as the rod of Jahveh's anger. If Assyria attacked Israel and Judah it was because Jahveh was using her to chastise His people. All nations were in Jahveh's hands to do with as He would. This was the great conviction of the eighth-century prophets – there is One God. He is God of History and not only the history of His chosen people, but the history of all people. There is only One God and He is Jahveh. This belief is what we call *Monotheism** – the belief that only one God exists. This God is the God of History and also the God of Nature because He is the Creator of all.

This, however, raises another question – what kind of God is He? The prophets maintain that He is righteous* and expects men to be righteous, too. Amos speaks for the poor – justice and mercy are demanded in the name of God because God is just and merciful. Hosea demands faithfulness and loyalty for the same reason. Isaiah and Micah give the same message. Jahveh is righteous and He demands righteousness from men. Syncretism is banned – polytheism is unthinkable and monolatry has perished. The belief has a practical implication. Because Jahveh is righteous and expects men to be righteous, He will punish men and nations if they are unrighteous and bless them if they are righteous.

The faith of the prophets is called *Ethical Monotheism* which means belief in One Righteous God who demands righteousness in men. It is the great contribution of the eighth-century prophets to the religion of the world.

Now let us summarise the message of the eighth-century prophets.

1. There is One God supreme in History. All nations are in the hollow of His hand. All human problems are subject to divine providence. God reigns in all the world and not over Israel and Judah only. Assyria, Egypt, Babylon are all under God's control. He not only works in spite of them but through them.

2. All the prophets had a passion for righteousness. This caused a good deal of their suffering and in some cases their martyrdom. They were again and again the conscience of the nation. They had seen that a righteous God demanded righteousness in His people and they thundered against sin wherever they found it.

3. The prophets attacked the sacrificial system, not because it was wrong, but because those who took part in it were insincere. However effective the sacrificial system was when it was linked with sincere worship, it was but a sham when treated as a formality. The prophets insisted on the sincere worship of God. They were against all cant and hypocrisy in religion.

4. The prophets spoke of the certainty of judgment. Again and again, with breaking hearts they had to prophesy the downfall of the nation. Continued sin must be and would be punished. The downfall of the nation was inevitable because of the way the nation was living. They saw with clearness from which direction the punishment must inevitably come. So in all of them there is the warning of judgment. The only escape from the punishment is 'Let the wicked forsake his way. . . .'

5. There was, however, one magnificent hope. They saw God not only as judge but as Redeemer and Saviour. They remembered His grace in past days, how He had led His people in every situation, and from this looking back over the past they gained confidence for the future. Doom and destruction are not the last words in any of the prophets. Beyond the suffering there is hope.

6. Isaiah's supreme message was of the Holiness of God. The word 'holy' originally meant 'separated'. God was holy because in His greatness He was separated from man. When anything belonged to God it was called 'holy' because it was His alone, so we read of the 'holy place'. God had chosen Israel to be His people and therefore they must be 'separate' from all others – a 'holy people'. The message of the prophets to Israel therefore was that above all else she must remember she belonged to God.

Summary 760-700 BC

Monolatry – there are many gods but Israel must worship only Jahveh.

Syncretism – the mixing of religious practices.

Ethical Monotheism – the message of the eighth-century prophets.

    a. There is One God who is Creator and Supreme in History.

    b. A Righteous God demands righteousness in His people.

    c. Worship must be sincere.

    d. Judgment inevitably follows disobedience.

    e. God is Redeemer and Saviour. Beyond the judgment there is hope.

    f. A Holy God must have a holy people.

Question

What contribution did the eighth-century prophets in Israel and Judah make to the development of religion?

CHAPTER 18

Manasseh

To study: II Kings 21

Manasseh (687-642) is regarded as the greatest villain amongst all the kings who occupied the throne of David. He reversed all the religious reforms of Hezekiah and his reign is pictured by the writer as the darkest period of Judah's history.

Let us look first of all at the situation in the wider world. Sennacherib was murdered and was succeeded by Esarhaddon (681-669) who began his reign by putting down a rebellion and then marched into Egypt, where he succeeded in taking Memphis. He was succeeded in 669 by Ashurbanipal. During the first part of his reign Assyria held undisputed sway over the whole of her empire. Ashurbanipal was one of the greatest of Assyria's kings. He was interested not only in war, but in literature, and one of the great discoveries of archaeology has been the library that he collected. He had to face a revolt in the province of Babylonia in 652 but he soon restored order. It was, however, an omen of things to come. The Egyptians rebelled and threw the Assyrians out of Egypt. Invaders were pouring into Mesopotamia from the north beyond the mountains and the great Median empire was becoming stronger. Despite Assyria's strength there were signs that the Empire was beginning to break up.

Manasseh's reign must be seen against this background. He remained a loyal vassal of Assyria throughout his reign and for that reason Judah was left alone during the periods of rebellion elsewhere. There is a story in the *Book of Chronicles* (II Chron 33 *11-13*) of how he was once taken in chains before the Assyrian king for suspected disloyalty but he was treated kindly and later restored to his throne. A prayer he is supposed to have prayed at this time is found in the *Apocrypha*. The truth of this story, however, is extremely doubtful.

Manasseh's general policy at home represented a complete break with Hezekiah and all that he stood for. The local shrines of Jahveh were restored. Pagan cults and practices were allowed to flourish and we get a return to the Canaanite fertility religion, with an Asherah and sacred prostitution. It seemed to be an attempt to amalgamate the religion of Jahveh with that of Baal.

Manasseh also paid homage to the Assyrian gods and erected altars to the Assyrian deities in the Temple. The Assyrian worship of the stars was practised. The reason behind this was of course political. A vassal state was expected to pay homage to the gods of the overlord. Nevertheless, the idea of pagan altars in the Jewish Temple caused horror to the loyal worshipper of Jahveh.

In addition to this pagan worship Manasseh reintroduced the practice of divination and magic. Foreign fashions were encouraged. Perhaps worst of all in the eyes of the faithful was his revival of the practice of human sacrifice and the cult of the dead.

The account given in *II Kings* suggests that Manasseh had a complete contempt for Jahveh's law. His reign was characterised by injustice and violence and he 'shed much innocent blood'. The adherents of the prophetic party were persecuted and tradition says that Isaiah was murdered during this reign.

One cannot help seeing the similarity between the reign of Manasseh and that of Ahab except that in the reign of Manasseh no prophet of the stature of Elijah arose to rebuke him, or, if he did, there is no record of him.

We must not suppose, however, that the supporters of Hezekiah and the prophets were idle even if they had to 'go underground'. Many people would probably be quite happy to support Manasseh, realising that his policy of subservience to Assyria gave them immunity from outside attack. On the other hand, there were many who deeply resented his policy. There were the nationalists who strongly opposed the dependence upon Assyria, and there were the sincere devotees of Jahveh who kept the faith alive in dark times. When in Josiah's time the opportunity came for a return to the loyal worship of Jahveh, there were many who were eager to support it.

Manasseh was succeeded in 642 by his son *Amon*, who followed the policy of his father. His reign was short, however. He was assassinated after two years during a patriotic revolt and he has no importance in the story we are following.

Summary   687-642 BC

Manasseh *a*. A vassal of Assyria.

b. Reverses domestic policy of Hezekiah.

c. Assyrian gods introduced and fertility cults restored.

d. Divination and magic.

e. Human sacrifice and the cult of the dead.

Amon

Question

'Manasseh is the villain amongst the kings of Judah, according to the writer of *II Kings*.' Discuss this statement.

CHAPTER 19

Josiah

To study: II Kings 22, 23

We have seen that during the reign of Manasseh the Assyrian Empire was beginning to crumble. That process was hastening in Josiah's reign and in 612 BC Nineveh was destroyed. *Josiah* (640-609) came to the throne when he was eight years old and we know nothing of the years when he was still a child. During his reign, however, Judah became once more completely independent and every sign of Assyrian domination was removed. He even extended his influence into the area which had once been the Northern Kingdom; in fact it seems as though he hoped for a united kingdom again. His reign is characterised by nationalism accompanied by religious reform and he is one of the really important kings of Judah. He is a king of whom the Biblical writer has nothing but good to say.

According to the book of *Kings* Josiah's reform began in his eighteenth year. It overshadows everything else he did and we hear little else about him apart from this reform. The launching of the reform is told in detail in *II Kings* 22 *3* to 23 *25*, and you should study this section carefully. It took place about the year 622 and began when, in the course of repairs to the Temple, a copy of the 'Book of the Law' was found. Make sure you know the story as it is told in *II Kings* 22 *1-20*. This 'Book of the Law' was brought to the attention of the King and the reading of it troubled him greatly. He consulted the prophetess Huldah to verify the truth of the word and then summoned the elders of the people to hear the law read. He then made a Covenant with Jahveh to obey this law.

It was from this that the great movement for reform began. Its main features were:

a. A consistent purge of all foreign cults and practices.

b. An extension of reform to the north.

c. All worship was centralised in Jerusalem and the rural priests were invited to come and take their place with the Temple priests.

d. The Passover was reinstituted. This was to restore the distinctive element in Israel's faith and marked the final break with Assyria. The reform marked a serious effort to recover the ideals and Covenant of the past.

Now let us look at Josiah's reforms in more detail. They are not easy to remember as they stand in the book of *Kings*. If, however, you group them together under the headings of Temple, around the Temple, and the Land, you will find it easier. First of all, then, the reforms associated with *the Temple*.

1. The vessels associated with the worship of Baal and the host of heaven were burned. The 'host of heaven' is a reference to the Assyrian worship of the sun, moon and stars.

2. The idolatrous priests were put down.

3. The Asherim were burned.

4. The pagan altars were broken down.

5. All images were broken.

6. The Passover was to be kept and worship centralised at Jerusalem.

Now for *the area surrounding the Temple*.

7. He broke down the houses of the sodomites and prostitutes – these were connected with the fertility worship.

8. The horses and chariots of the sun were destroyed – these again were associated with Assyrian worship.

110

9. The wizards and those who had familiar spirits were put away. This was the destroying of divination and the cult of the dead.

And, finally, *the rest of the land.*

10. All high places were defiled.

11. The valley of Hinnom* – the place of human sacrifice – was defiled so that no human sacrifice should ever be offered again.

12. The altar at Bethel was broken down.

13. The high places of Samaria were destroyed and their priests slain.

The climax of the reformation came with the celebration of a great Passover of which the writer tells us 'there was not such a passover from the days of the judges that judged Israel.'

Behind this story lies an interesting question – What was the law book found in the Temple upon which the reformation was based? Most scholars now agree that it was some form of the *Book of Deuteronomy*, especially Chapters 12 to 26. There are many reasons for thinking this to be the case, the most obvious one being that the reforms of Josiah are in accordance with the precepts of *Deuteronomy*. Notice the following comparisons:

1. The Asherim are destroyed in *II Kings* 23 *4, 6, 14-15*; cf. *Deuteronomy* 12 *3.*

2. The worship of the heavenly host is forbidden in *II Kings* 23 *4*;
cf. *Deuteronomy* 17 *3.*

3. The high places are profaned and abolished in *II Kings* 23 *8*;
cf. *Deuteronomy* 12 *2-5.*

4. Moloch worship and child burning are abolished in *II Kings* 23 10;
cf. *Deuteronomy* 18 *10.*

111

5. Wizards are suppressed in *II Kings* 23 *24*; cf. *Deuteronomy* 18 *10-11*.

6. Passover is to be celebrated only at Jerusalem whereas formerly it has been celebrated locally. *II Kings* 23 *21-23*; cf. *Deuteronomy* 16 *1-7*.

You will see that Josiah seems to be carrying out to the letter the laws found in the *Book of Deuteronomy*. It is to this book that we shall turn in our next chapter.

Summary   640–609 BC

Josiah *a.* Becomes independent of Assyria.

      b. A time of nationalism and religious reform.

      c. The discovery of the 'Book of the Law'.

Josiah's reforms

In the Temple

      a. Vessels associated with Baal destroyed.

      b. Priests associated with the worship of idols to be put down.

      c. Asherim burned.

      d. Pagan altars broken down.

      e. Images broken.

      f. Passover to be kept.

Around the Temple

      a. Houses of sodomites and prostitutes destroyed.

      b. Horses and chariots of the sun destroyed.

      c. Wizards and those with familiar spirits put away.

In the Land

      a. All high places defiled.

      b. Valley of Hinnom defiled.

      c. Altar at Bethel broken down.

      d. High places of Samaria destroyed and priests slain.

ALL WORSHIP CENTRALISED IN JERUSALEM.

Question

Compare the reforms of Josiah with those of Hezekiah.

CHAPTER 20

The Book of Deuteronomy

When Josiah introduced his reforms into Judah, religion was based upon a book for the first time. The *Book of Deuteronomy* not only inspired the reforms of Josiah, it greatly influenced later prophets and historians and is quoted more than eighty times in the New Testament, more than any other Old Testament book. It is necessary, therefore, that we should look at it and see from whence came this long line of influence.

It is a book which would instruct the Israelite in the ordinary duties of his life. It gives directions for feasts and offerings, rules concerning sacrifice and the general principles of family life. Justice must be equal for all and the kings must always remember that Israel is first of all ruled by God.

But this is more than a mere code of laws. It is inspired by a real sense of the meaning of true religion and of the need for it to be expressed in right conduct. The author reminds Israel of her privileges and the Covenant. He emphasises the love of God and traces the suffering of Israel to God correcting them as a father should. Duties are to be performed not from fear, but as the outcome of a personal devotion to God. In fact, Love of God is to become the motive of human action.

Deuteronomy has often been quoted for its humanitarian emphasis. All men are equal before the law and there must be no exploitation of one by another. Social justice is most important. Jahveh stands by the weak, the helpless, the orphan, the widow, the resident alien, and so must Israel. An illustration of this is to be found in the regulations regarding harvesting in *Deuteronomy* 24 *19-22*. Some of the wheat or the fruit must always be left for the widow, the fatherless and the stranger. *Deuteronomy*, which literally means 'second law', is written in the form of discourses which Moses is supposed to have given to Israel just before they entered into the Promised Land. It was quite a common thing to use the name of a great figure of the past to give authority to a work, so we need spend no time in discussing the question of authorship. We will draw your attention to some sections which are most important for your purpose.

The first discourse, which comprises Chapters 1 to 4, draws lessons for the present from the past. God's goodness in the wilderness is described and cities of refuge are appointed.

The second discourse (5 to 26) contains laws for the present. There is first of all a repetition of the Ten Commandments and then an exhortation to keep them. In Chapter 6 verses *4* and *5* we have what is called the 'Shema' which was regarded by the Rabbis and by Jesus as a summary of the Law and is still repeated by faithful Jews today. Other important parts of this section are as follows:

> The centralising of worship. 12 *1-14*.
> The three Jewish Feasts. 16 *1-17*.
> Treatment of the poor. 15 *1-3, 7-11*; 24 *17-22*.
> Treatment of slaves. 15 *12-18*; 23 *15-16*.
> Fair weights and measures. 25 *13-16*.

There are three shorter discourses in Chapters 27 to 31 exhorting Israel for the future and pronouncing curses and blessings according as the Law is kept. The book ends with the Song and Blessing of Moses and an account of his death.

This then was the book upon which the great reformation was based. We have now to consider the results of the reformation. There is no doubt that at first Josiah's reformation made a great impression. The fact that the viewpoint of the historian is moulded by it is sufficient evidence of this. It seemed like the dawn of a new age for Judah when, in renewed Covenant with her God, she could go forward to greater things. It has to be remembered, however, that the reform was largely inspired by the desire for political independence and that it was only possible because of the declining power of Assyria. One cannot imagine all traces of Assyrian domination in worship being removed if Assyria had not been too busily occupied elsewhere to intervene.

There were also great weaknesses, as Jeremiah later emphasised. The reformation was imposed from above upon a people who were not reforming in spirit. It was a purely external thing. A set of new laws had been published and they had to be kept. The fact of keeping the laws made the people feel that they were doing Jahveh's will and all would be well. The centralising of worship at Jerusalem made people feel secure. Jahveh was now in their midst and no harm could come to them. A superficial reform brought an unfounded sense of security.

The idea behind the reformation was also inadequate. The theme was – obey these laws and all will be well with us; disobey and we shall be punished. Apart from the fact that this made religion a kind of 'insurance policy', it was altogether too simple a reading of the situation. Josiah undoubtedly meant well but, as Jeremiah saw, the reform did not go deep enough.

Outside events soon made their presence felt and brought great disillusionment. Assyria was tottering to a fall. She had many enemies and the most dangerous of these was Babylon. As Assyria was being attacked from many sides, Pharaoh Necho of Egypt decided to come to her assistance. Assyria had been the enemy of Egypt but Pharaoh Necho realised that Assyria was no longer a great power. She could, however, be a useful 'buffer-state' between himself and Babylon. To go to the help of Assyria now would also give him the excuse to bring Palestine and Syria under Egyptian influence. Nineveh had fallen in 612. Pharaoh Necho set out with a large force to go to Carchemish on the River Euphrates, to strengthen the weakening power of Assyria and to help her to retake some of her territory from the Babylonians (609 BC).

Josiah had also been studying the signs of the times and decided to throw in his lot with Babylon. He intercepted Pharaoh Necho in his march at Megiddo*. Necho defeated and executed him and then marched on to challenge the might of Babylon at Carchemish.

The result of this important encounter was that Necho was hopelessly beaten at Carchemish (605 BC) by Nebuchadrezzar of Babylon. This may have been partly due to the delay caused by his encounter with Josiah, and also to the fact that the battle with Josiah's forces had weakened his army. The Egyptians fled in disorder after what was to be their last attempt to establish an empire in the Fertile Crescent, and Babylon was the new mistress of the world.

This was a tremendous blow to Judah. Her king was killed. The reform he instituted lasted less than twenty years and then all of it was destroyed.

Summary
c. 622 BC

Deuteronomy: The 'Second Law'.

- *a.* The religion of a book.
- *b.* A code of laws for a nation ruled by God.
- *c.* The motive for keeping the law is to be gratitude and love to God, and therefore to men.
- *d.* Characterised by social justice and humanity.

Results of the Reformation

- *a.* A sincere attempt to return to the Covenant.
- *b.* The weaknesses were in its external nature.
- *c.* Centralising of worship gave false sense of security.
- *d.* The reform did not go deep enough.

The Rise of Babylon

Josiah executed by Pharaoh-Necho.

Carchemish.

Question

Summarise the weaknesses of the Deuteronomic reformation.

CHAPTER 21

The Fall of Judah

To study: II Kings 23 *31* to 25

We now have to master a rather confusing period of history. Let us recall the situation. Assyria was crumbling as an empire and the great question was 'Who is going to take her place?' Nabopolassar, vassal king of Babylon, had revolted and made himself independent in the lower part of Mesopotamia. Egypt had always had ambitions of ruling the world. The empire of Media, to the north-east of the Mesopotamian area was growing in strength under the leadership of Kyaxares. The situation was made even more complicated by the invasion of the Scythian hordes. These were nomads from Central Asia who swept down upon the Fertile Crescent seeking new pastures. It was they who finally sacked Nineveh in 612 BC.

For twenty years there was confusion as each contender for supremacy built up strength. Egypt tried to support Assyria, as we have seen, in order to stave off the threat from Babylon. The battle of Carchemish in 605 settled the issue. Necho was defeated by Nabopolassar's son, Nebuchadrezzar, and Babylon became mistress of the world. She now controlled the whole of the Assyrian Empire as far as the Egyptian frontier. The Median Empire had power in the north but Media and Babylon did not come into conflict.

So far as Judah was concerned we have seen that her king, Josiah, was killed by Pharaoh Necho at Megiddo. The people made his son, *Jehoahaz*, king. He was not,

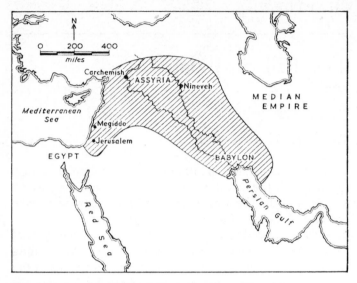

The clash of empires – Who shall take the place of Assyria?
Babylonian Empire shaded

however, too sympathetic to Egypt and as Judah was
largely in the power of Egypt at this juncture he was de-
posed. He was taken as a prisoner to Egypt, where he died.

The Egyptians placed his brother, *Jehoiakim*, on the
throne. He was obviously more amenable to Egypt. We
do not read much about him in the book of *Kings*; we
shall meet him again when we come to consider Jeremiah.
All we are told is that he had to face some border raids
from various neighbouring countries. He was very much
under the influence of Egypt who, although her power had
been broken by Babylon, was still able to stir up trouble.
Encouraged by Egypt he revolted against Babylon to whom
he had become tributary. Babylon immediately reacted
by attacking and besieging Jerusalem.

Jehoiakim died before the city was taken and was succeeded by his son, *Jehoiachin*, who was only eighteen. He

only reigned for three months, at the end of which he was compelled to surrender the city to Nebuchadrezzar and he was carried off to captivity in Babylon.

Judah suffered greatly because of the rebellion of Jehoiakim. Many of her cities were badly damaged. Nebuchadrezzar deported to Babylon all those whom he thought likely to cause him trouble, and they included most of the able leaders of the people. In place of Jehoiachin, Babylon placed Zedekiah* on the throne as a kind of puppet king. This was in 597 BC.

Zedekiah had a very difficult task. He was not a strong personality and although he meant well he could not stand up to the intrigues of his courtiers. He was much afraid of the opinion of the people. His authority was undermined by the fact that Jehoiachin was being treated as a royal prisoner in Babylon and was regarded by many as the legitimate king. He was short of leaders who were inspired by motives other than those of self-interest.

During this period a rebellion broke out in Babylon in which some of the deported Jews seem to have been involved. Some of their prophets were executed by Nebuchadrezzar, who had no difficulty in putting down the revolt. News of this rebellion reached Palestine and raised the hopes of many people. Neighbouring tribes from Edom, Moab, Tyre and Sidon sent embassies to Jerusalem to discuss the possibility of revolt. False prophets incited the people saying that Jahveh was about to break the yoke of the King of Babylon and that within two years Jehoiachin and the exiles would return in triumph to Jerusalem. Jeremiah denounced these prophecies and even wrote a letter to the exiles telling them to settle in Babylon for a long stay. The rebellion came to nothing and Zedekiah sent word to Nebuchadrezzar assuring him of his loyalty.

The spirit of rebellion, however, did not disappear. It is not easy to trace the steps which led to the final decision. Egypt was certainly one influence, but no other states in

Palestine seemed to have joined in. Zedekiah was not certain what to do, but in the end he could not withstand the pressure of those about him who were eager for rebellion. He withheld tribute from Babylon and Babylon struck quickly.

The Babylonian army laid siege to Jerusalem and began to destroy the outlying strongholds until only Lachish and Azekah were left. An Egyptian army advanced to relieve the city and for a time hopes were raised, but the Egyptians were quickly driven back. Jerusalem held out from January until mid-summer, but at last, in July 587, when the city's food supply was exhausted, the Babylonians breached the city walls and poured in. Zedekiah fled in the night, hoping to reach safety in Ammon. He was captured near Jericho and taken before Nebuchadrezzar at his headquarters in Riblah. The king of Babylon showed no mercy. He forced Zedekiah to witness the execution of his sons, then put out his eyes and led him in captivity to Babylon. There he died.

A month later Nebuchadrezzar ordered his commander, Nebuzaradan, to set fire to the city of Jerusalem and level its walls. Many leading citizens were executed and some deported (586 BC).

Judah was now organised as a province of the empire. A Governor was appointed instead of a king. The man appointed was Gedaliah, a man of noble family in Jerusalem. He tried to build up his people and to reconcile them to their fate, hoping to preserve something of Judah's inheritance. He realised that the only way was to work with Babylon. He was, however, regarded as a 'collaborationist' and a plot to kill him was worked out by Ishmael, a member of the royal family, helped by the king of Ammon. Gedaliah was warned of the plot but was too noble a soul to believe in it. Ishmael struck him down and fled to Ammon. Gedaliah's friends feared the vengeance of Nebuchadrezzar and fled to Egypt, taking Jeremiah with them.

Jeremiah mentions a third deportation in 582. This was possibly a reprisal for the murder of Gedaliah. The province of Judah was now abolished and she became part of the neighbouring province of Samaria. The kingdom had gone and nothing remained in Palestine.

Now read carefully the chapters in *II Kings* which are given at the head of this chapter. The period is confusing but the stories are not too difficult to remember.

Summary   608-586 BC

Jehoahaz	Deposed by Necho.
Jehoiakim	Encouraged by Egypt, revolts against Babylon.
Jehoiachin	Surrenders to Babylon.

First Deportation, 597.

Zedekiah
  a. Weak, easily influenced, no reliable leaders.
  b. Rebellion in Babylon encourages false hopes.
  c. Zedekiah witholds tribute.
  d. Siege of Jerusalem.

Second Deportation, 586.

Gedaliah   Made governor, assassinated by Ishmael.
Province of Judah abolished.

Question

Write notes on Gedaliah; Zedekiah; Jehoiakim; Nabopolassar.

Kings of Judah
after the fall of Samaria

BC	Kings	Prophets	Assyria
715	*Hezekiah*	*Isaiah*	Sennacherib
687	*Manasseh*	*Micah*	
642	*Amon*		
640	*Josiah*		
			Fall of Nineveh 612
609	*Jehoahaz* (3 months)		*Babylon Supreme*
609	*Jehoiakim*	*Jeremiah*	
			Carchemish 605
598	*Jehoiachin* (3 months)		Nebuchadrezzar
597	*Zedekiah*	*First deportation 597*	
586	Gedaliah	*Second deportation 586*	
		Third deportation 582?	

CHAPTER 22

Jeremiah

Jeremiah was one of the greatest prophets of Judah. Some would describe him as the greatest prophet before the Exile. His book is a long one and there is much in it that you ought to know. In this chapter we shall think about his call and some of the incidents in his life. In the next chapter we shall consider his message. Read the chapters in the book of Jeremiah to which we refer, together with the notes we give upon them.

The background of the ministry of Jeremiah was the period from the reign of Josiah to the fall of Jerusalem. It was a period of great empires struggling for mastery, with the smaller nations often regarded as pawns in the game. One crisis followed another. It was a time of mounting tragedy for Judah.

Jeremiah was born about 650 BC at Anathoth, a village about 3 miles north-east of Jerusalem. About 626 he was called by God to be a prophet. How far he identified himself with the reforms of Josiah is uncertain. He saw that they were insufficient and preached instead a religion of the heart and proclaimed that the rebirth of the nation must be worked out in terms of right dealings between men.

Chapter 1. The call and commission of Jeremiah. In verses 4 to 10 we get the story of how God called Jeremiah. Jeremiah hesitated to respond because of his youth – 'How can one so young go to others?' But God replied that before his birth He had intended him for a prophet. Jeremiah was to be a living voice to proclaim God's will to the nations. Compare this call with the call of Isaiah.

In verses *4* to *19* we are shown how God's word came to Jeremiah.

(*a*) *The Almond Tree.* This is the first tree to betoken the coming of spring. It looks bare and then breaks out into flowers. It has appeared dead but all the time life has been working in the tree. So God tells Jeremiah that He is awake and will bring His word to pass.

(*b*) *The Boiling Pot.* Jeremiah sees a boiling pot tilted over so that the liquid pours out. It is tilted over from the north. This symbolises the certainty of judgment from the north. Judah is to be invaded. The warning sign appears just as the Assyrian empire is tottering. Many scholars think that Jeremiah was referring to the Scythian hordes who were sweeping into the Fertile Crescent.

Chapter 19. Jeremiah was told to buy a potter's earthen flask. Once broken this could never be used again. It was so delicate and precious that it could not be mended. He was told to take with him elders and senior priests and go to the Potsherd Gate – the place where rubbish was dumped. There he had to break the flask in the sight of witnesses. This had a double message – Judah was precious to her maker but her sin had hardened her beyond repair and she would have to be broken.

After breaking the flask and giving the message, Jeremiah went to the Temple Court and repeated his pronouncement.

Chapter 20. Pashur the priest, who was overseer of the Temple, arrested Jeremiah when he heard his proclamation in the Temple court. He beat him and placed him in the stocks. There he was exposed to the insults of the public and he was left there until the following night. When Pashur came to release him Jeremiah told him that the Lord was going to give him a new name, 'Terror on every side'. The king of Babylon would execute judgment on the Holy City. The spoil would include both the treasures of

Jerusalem and its people. Pashur himself would be taken captive and see his friends perish by the sword.

Chapter 21 *1-10*. This chapter refers to the siege of Jerusalem during the reign of Zedekiah. The Pashur referred to here is not the same man as in Chapter 20. At this point Jeremiah is not the persecuted prophet but the elder statesman whose advice is sought by the king. Zedekiah was hoping to escape from the clutches of Nebuchadrezzar and sent to Jeremiah to seek God's favour. Jeremiah could offer the king no hope after he had rejected earlier warnings. God would support the besieger and deliver Zedekiah and the survivors to the enemy. Jeremiah was reaffirming here the policy he had advocated from the beginning. Zedekiah had made an oath of loyalty to Nebuchadrezzar, yet he had conspired with Egypt against him and must pay the penalty.

Chapter 26. Jeremiah preached a sermon in the Temple. We shall refer to this in more detail when we come to consider his message. After the sermon he was arrested. His crime was that he had suggested that the Temple could fall. This went against the religious and patriotic principles of the people and the cry went up, 'You shall die'. The priests and prophets arrested him. The princes and officials of the court then appeared on the scene. He had an opportunity to defend himself and told them that the Lord had sent him. If they would amend their ways, the dire consequences would not come to pass. He convinced the princes and the people. Jeremiah was released and placed under the protection of Ahikam, a man of influence.

We are not told what the king's attitude was at this time, but in verses *20-24* we are given an illustration of his treatment of another prophet, which promises ill for Jeremiah.

Chapter 28. We referred in the last chapter to the occasion when a rebellion in Babylon aroused hopes in Judah.

Now we are told of how a false prophet, Hananiah, proclaimed that Jahveh was about to deliver His people from the power of Babylon. Jeremiah had been going about with a wooden yoke on his shoulders as a sign of submission to Babylon. Hananiah contemptuously broke the yoke but Jeremiah replaced it with one of iron. In the next chapter we are told how Jeremiah sent a letter to the people in exile advising them to settle down and make their home in Babylon for they were not coming back for a long time.

Chapter 34. The Babylonian army had invaded Palestine and Jeremiah gave advice to king Zedekiah. During the siege, when things were at their worst, liberty was proclaimed to the slaves, perhaps to gain extra men to defend the ramparts and also to avoid the slaves turning against their masters if the walls were breached. Then there was a lull in the fighting and the Egyptian army had come to draw off the Babylonians. Things seemed to be more hopeful. The slaves were taken back into slavery. Jeremiah proclaimed 'liberty to the sword'.

The background of verses *12-22* is as follows. According to *Deuteronomy* 15 *12-15*, no Hebrew was to enslave a brother Hebrew permanently. He might use his brother's services for a period of six years, then he must set him free. This practice had been neglected. With the siege of the city the people had repented and sealed their action in the Temple. They had used a service which had been used centuries before. It involved passing between the parts of a calf which had been cut in two. Now they had broken their solemn covenant with God. Jeremiah denounced them. They had not only wronged their fellows but had profaned the divine name. They would be given into the hands of their enemies.

Chapter 35. We hear of the Rechabites* again. Jeremiah brings them into the Temple and asks them to drink wine. They refuse. They say they have only come into the city

128

at all because of the besieging armies. They will not be unfaithful to their fathers by breaking their vows of abstinence. Jeremiah uses them as an illustration. They will be loyal to their fathers long dead but Judah will not be loyal to her God.

Chapter 36. Jeremiah dictates his message which is written on a scroll and his scribe, Baruch, goes and reads it in the court of the Temple. It is reported to the princes – the responsible Temple officials. Baruch is taken into the secretary's chamber and asked to read it to the princes. They are afraid at the message and decide to report to the king. At the same time they warn Baruch to hide himself and his master. The scroll is taken to king Jehoiakim who is sitting in the winter house before the fire. As the scroll is read he cuts off portions and throws them into the fire. Some of the princes urge him not to burn it but he does not fear the message. Jehoiakim orders the arrest of Jeremiah and Baruch but they are hidden. Another scroll is written and enlarged, and this includes a further warning to Jehoiakim. Many scholars think that the contents of this second scroll are to be found in Chapters 1 to 20 of the present book.

Chapter 38. After an interview with Zedekiah described in Chapter 37, Jeremiah, still a prisoner, was taken into the palace area for his imprisonment. The imprisonment was not strict and Jeremiah used the opportunity to keep in touch with the public and urge them to desert to the enemy. This was interpreted as treason although it was only continuing his original message. Zedekiah had broken his oath to Nebuchadrezzar. Jeremiah would not break his oath to the Lord.

He was reported to the Temple officials and judged worthy of death. The weak king would not kill him outright so he allowed him to be lowered by ropes into the disused cistern in the palace yard. There he was left to lie in the mud without food and would have died if it had not been for a black slave, Ebed-melech, who rescued him.

Chapters 39 and 40 *1-6*. We get another description of the fall of Jerusalem. You will notice that when Nebucha-drezzar takes the city he gives Jeremiah the choice as to where he will live. He can go and live in comfort in Babylon or remain in Jerusalem. Jeremiah chooses to remain with his people.

Summary   *c*. 650-580 BC

Incidents in the life of Jeremiah

a. The Call: the Almond Tree: the Cauldron (1).

b. He breaks the potter's flask (19).

c. He is put in the stocks by Pashur (20).

d. Advises Zedekiah (21).

e. Arrested after Temple Sermon (26).

f. Dispute with Hananiah (28).

g. Advises Zedekiah and the freeing of the slaves (34).

h. The Rechabites (35).

i. The burning of the Scroll (36).

j. Rescued from the cistern (38).

k. The fall of Jerusalem (39, 40).

Questions

---

1. Relate the stories of the calls of the two prophets Isaiah and Jeremiah. In what ways do these accounts throw light upon the difference in character and temperament between the two men?

2. Select any three incidents in the life of Jeremiah and write brief accounts of them.

3. Write notes on: Pashur the priest; Baruch; Hananiah; Ebed-melech.

CHAPTER 23

The Message of Jeremiah

We have seen that Jeremiah was called to prophesy during the reign of Josiah. His attitude to that king's reforms might have been enthusiastic at first but he soon saw that the reform was too superficial to accomplish anything permanent. His attitude can be judged from 3 *6-10* where he says that Judah did not return to the Lord with her whole heart.

We have now to consider the message of Jeremiah and first of all we shall think of his general message, and then turn to the special word that he alone of the prophets gave.

Jeremiah's general message can be seen from the early chapters of his book. A more detailed comment on these chapters is given in the Appendix to this chapter. The theme of Chapters 2 and 3 is that God chose His people, the Covenant was a marriage bond, and God gave them the land in which they dwell. Despite this they have forgotten their God. Even their leaders fail and are denounced as 'unworthy shepherds'. They must bear in mind what had happened to Israel. If they persist in turning away from God the same fate will come to them. Notice particularly the illustrations which Jeremiah uses to drive this message home. The chief of these are as follows:

2 *13*. Here Jeremiah says that the people have forsaken the fountain of living waters and hewn out cisterns which are broken. 'Living water' is the water of the stream, fresh and pure. The water of the cistern is stagnant and can breed disease and death.

2 *21*. Israel is a vine which has degenerated. Notice this symbol of the vine referring to Israel. Isaiah used it in his parable of the vine, and Jesus used it in his discourse to the disciples in the upper room. The vine was a favourite symbol for Israel.

2 *22*. Israel is so filthy that no soap can clean her.

2 *24-25*. Here is a very scathing reference. Israel is like a wild ass in heat pursuing other lovers. We have noticed before the picture of Israel's relationship with Jahveh as a marriage. When she turns away from Jahveh she is described as going after other lovers. In this case Jeremiah says that any lovers will do. A similar picture is used in Chapter 3 where Israel is described as a faithless wife.

5 *1-5*. Here Jeremiah goes through the city trying to find an upright man. He goes first of all to the ordinary people and cannot find one who is good. Then he thinks that perhaps he has been looking in the wrong place. He will go to the great and speak to them. Again his search is fruitless. There is not one righteous man in Jerusalem.

6 *9*. When judgment comes it will be thorough. The picture is of a vineyard at harvest-time. The law said that some fruit must always be left for the gleaners. When they had finished nothing would be left. Judah is to be like a gleaned vineyard.

Jeremiah summed up his message in his famous Temple Sermon. This is given in full in Chapter 7 and summarised in Chapter 26. In outline it was as follows:—

1. There is no security in the Temple worship.

2. Security for Judah depends upon justice in the land and the absence of oppression.

3. Formal worship will not fulfil her responsibilities to Jahveh.

4. God can dispense with the Temple.

5. God demands obedience and not sacrifice.

6. The people have been warned – God will destroy.

Jeremiah's message so far is very similar to that of the prophets who have gone before him. It is the theme of them all – the God of righteousness demanding righteousness and justice and preparing to bring judgment on those who betray the Covenant. But Jeremiah goes further than others. There are two themes on which he takes a completely new line and they are both found in Chapter 31.

1. *Individual Responsibility.* 31 *29-30*

It is a common thing for any generation to blame its troubles upon the sins of the generation which has gone before it. The Hebrews were particularly inclined to do this. We must remember that they had a belief in the solidarity of the race which is not always easy for us to understand. A man and his family stood together and if a man sinned, his family had to take the consequences. They saw nothing unjust in this. If a man sinned, his descendants also had to pay the penalty of his sin. There was a proverb which summed up this idea, 'The fathers have eaten sour grapes and the children's teeth are set on edge.' It was the equivalent of the belief that God visited the sins of the fathers upon the children unto the third and fourth generation. The people who had gone into exile after the fall of Jerusalem had quoted this proverb and blamed their predicament upon the sins of their fathers. Jeremiah quotes this proverb as he points to a new order. In future every individual will be accountable to God personally. Men shall no more quote this proverb. The man who eats the sour grapes will have his own teeth set on edge. Ezekiel was also to quote this proverb and to develop Jeremiah's doctrine still further.

It was, however, Jeremiah who first proclaimed the message of individual responsibility before God, and, if we accept it as obvious today, it is because Jeremiah's message has gone home.

2. *The New Covenant*. 31 *31-34*

Jeremiah's greatest contribution, however, was in his message of the New Covenant. This passage is one that you should know by heart. It gives us the distinction between the Old and New Testaments in the Bible. It was in the mind of Jesus at the Last Supper. Read these verses very carefully. Notice the phrase 'Thus saith the Lord' occurs four times in these four verses. The Hebrew version implies that the prophet is in intimate touch with God as he proclaims these words. He is writing down the message as he receives it and it is a message with special authority behind it.

The Covenant is God taking the initiative. Notice the pronouns – *I* will put, *I* will write, *I* will be, *I* will forgive. In verse *32* we have another reference to the marriage idea of the Covenant, 'I was an husband.' At Sinai God had taken possession of His people. The relation is a personal one based on affection. God has been faithful although they have broken the Covenant. But now there is to be a new Covenant. Formerly they were called to obey the Law as their side of the Covenant. But the Law could not inspire; it was only a list of prohibited things. There was no real motive power behind it. Now notice the three promises of the New Covenant.

a. ' I will put My law within them.' God's claim will enter into a person's understanding. There is to be an expression of God's will within them. There is to be a union of wills – in other words, they will do God's will because they want to do it.

b. 'They shall all know Me.' God will no longer send messages to representatives like the prophets. He will speak directly. There will be no need for teachers in order that men shall know God, no need for intermediaries. 'They shall all know Me.'

c. 'I will forgive their iniquity.' The New Covenant will be possible because the guilt will be removed and a new sense of a man's worth will follow. He will then desire to be worthy and live in fellowhip with his God.

The statement of the New Covenant is followed by an assurance that this is as certain as the fact that God upholds nature. The city of Jerusalem will be rebuilt and God's people will once again be faithful.

A word must be said about Jeremiah's political message. During the reigns of Jehoiakim and Zedekiah he had one message only. He maintained that the only wise policy for Judah was to submit to Babylon. He knew that Judah would not do this and would seek to rebel at every opportunity, but he proclaimed again and again that rebellion would end in the fall of the city and the deportation of the people. He believed, however, that Israel would survive in exile.

This sounded like madness in the ears of the people. Had not Jahveh saved Jerusalem in the days of Isaiah? Would He not save it again? Jeremiah preached with a breaking heart that Jerusalem would not be saved this time. It was this message which brought him persecution. And yet he proclaimed that after exile the people would be restored. Even when Jerusalem was falling and the Babylonians were at the gates, he bought a field in Anathoth (32 *6-15*). The field was occupied by the besiegers but Jeremiah bought it to prove his confidence that 'houses and fields and vineyards shall again be bought in this land.'

He based his hope for the future on a new redemptive act of God. Jeremiah is sometimes described as a pessimist, indeed, to be a 'jeremiah' is to be a gloomy sort of person. He had to preach a message of gloom, but although he was pessimistic about the immediate future of the nation because he was a realist, he saw beyond the immediate future and looked forward with a great and triumphant hope.

Summary

The Message of Jeremiah

1. The Common Message of the Prophets

    a. God's choice of His people; the marriage bond of Covenant. The people have forgotten God and their leaders are unworthy (2, 3).

    b. Broken cisterns; degenerate vine (2); gleaned vineyard (6).

    c. Search for righteous man (5).

    d. The Temple Sermon (7, 26):

        i. Security not in the Temple but in justice.
        ii. God can dispense with the Temple.
        iii. God demands obedience not sacrifice.
        iv. God will destroy.

2. Original

    a. Individual responsibility (31).

    b. The New Covenant (31):

        i. The Law within.
        ii. All shall know Me.
        iii. I will forgive.

3. Political

    Submit to Babylon.

Questions

1. Write a short essay on the life and work of Jeremiah.

2. Discuss Jeremiah's doctrines of individual responsibility and the 'New Covenant'. In what sense were these new?

Appendix to 'The Message of Jeremiah'

The following notes will help you to study the message of Jeremiah as it is given in the first few chapters.

Chapter 2

verses 1–3. Jeremiah begins by recalling what had made Israel God's chosen people. Like Hosea he depicts the relationship in terms of the marriage bond. Israel was set aside to be the bride of God.

verses 4–8. But God's people had forgotten. They had forgotten how God had delivered them from Egypt, guided them in the wilderness and given them possession of the land. Their leaders, who should have sought God's will, had failed them. Four groups of people are described as faithless – the priests, the administrators of the law, the rulers and the prophets.

verses 9 to 13. Jeremiah asks his people to look from west to east, from Cyprus in the west to Kedar (an Arabian tribe), and consider that no nation forsakes the gods of its fathers easily. Yet God's people have left the source of all their blessings – the fount of living waters. They have hewed out worthless substitutes, idols, things they have made themselves, which like broken cisterns cannot sustain them.

verses 14–19. Think now of the fate that has overtaken Israel. Her ruined cities should serve as a warning. Egypt and Assyria have always despoiled other peoples. It is foolish to rely upon them rather than upon God. 'Lions' refers to Assyria. Part of Jeremiah's objection to foreign alliances was that they brought with them religious influences from other nations.

verses 20–28. A series of vivid pictures to show how Judah has deteriorated. From being a 'choice vine' she has become a degenerate plant. Her life is stained with marks that lye (or 'Nitre', a washing substance) and soap cannot remove. Her passion for mates other than her true husband has led her into unrestrained sin. Her thirst for the love of strangers is futile and fatal. To worship a tree or stone is a shameful thing. No such gods could save in time of trouble.

Note the comparisons in this section. Israel is compared to an animal that has broken its yoke (*20*), a harlot (*20*), a wild vine (*21*), a camel straying from the herd (*23*), a wild ass in heat (*24*), and a thief (*26*).

137

verses 29–37. Judah has no right to complain when God corrects His rebellious children. Has He been a wilderness to them or a land of thick darkness? Can a bride forget the thrill and finery of her wedding day? How can God's people be so forgetful and faithless? They have deliberately gone after many lovers. Two of these – Egypt and Assyria – have brought only shame and humiliation. How can they deny their guilt?

Chapter 3

verses 1–5. Like Hosea, Jeremiah now likens the people's sin to harlotry. Can they regard this without shame? No language of endearment (as in verse *4*) can hide their faithlessness. Their behaviour has betrayed them. It is no use seeking a casual return to Jahveh. Verse *3* reveals a common belief that Jahveh sometimes withheld the rain as a punishment for sin.

verses 6–14. He likens Israel to a faithless wife now divorced. The northern kingdom had sinned and was now in captivity because of it. Jahveh had cast her off. But Judah, her sister, is following her example. Although accepting the outward reforms under Josiah, she is only pretending. This makes her sin all the worse. But Jahveh still wants her to repent. Even Israel might yet be brought home if she would acknowledge her guilt and repent.

verses 15–25. The Covenant God still longs to bless and not punish His people. Jerusalem can still be brought to a position of eminence among the nations if she will repent and turn to Jahveh in sincerity. He will then give them shepherds (i.e. rulers) after his own heart. The voice of weeping and supplication will be the sign of a genuine return to God. God would then restore them to health. Their only help is in the God whom their fathers had disobeyed.

NOTE ON THE BOOKS OF *KINGS* AND *CHRONICLES*

There are two books of 'Chronicles' in our Bible which tell the history of this period. Do not confuse them with the *'Books of the Chronicles of the Kings of Israel and Judah'* which are referred to in *I and II Kings*. They were the court records and were probably destroyed in the fall of Jerusalem. They do not now exist.

The books of *I and II Chronicles* in our Bible are part of a later work of history. The writer of this work set out to tell the history of the world from a different point of view. He used and rewrote the story in *Samuel* and *Kings*. Originally this work contained four volumes – the two books of *Chronicles* together with *Ezra* and *Nehemiah*. It was published some time between 400 and 200 BC.

The writer was more concerned to teach religion than to be historically accurate. He was more a theologian than a scientific historian. This does not mean that his account is untrue – on the contrary it helps us by filling in many of the gaps in the story in the books of *Kings*. The story in *Chronicles* is largely centred on Judah, and Israel is only mentioned in order to tell Judah's story properly.

The section of 'Chronicles' which covers our period is found in *II Chronicles* Chapters 10 to 36. The following are the chief places where you will find it helpful to compare the *Kings* account with the account in *Chronicles*.

Abijah defeats Jeroboam	II Chronicles 13
Asa repulses the Ethiopians	14
Jehoshaphat's reign	17-20
Joash	24
Amaziah	25
Hezekiah	29-32
Manasseh	33

The Kings of Assyria (for reference only)

BC		
883	Ashurnasirpal II	overruns Mesopotamia to Tyre and Sidon.
859	Shalmaneser III	853. Battle of Qarqar against Western coalition. 841. Attacks Phoenicia. Tribute from Jehu.
823	Shamshiadad IV	
810	Adadnirari III	attacks and cripples Syria.
781	Shalmaneser IV	
771	Ashurdan III	
753	Ashurnirari V	
745	Tiglath-Pileser III	conquers Babylon. Uproots conquered peoples. Tribute from Menahem and Pekahiah. At appeal of Ahaz lays waste Damascus and organises as Syrian province. Hoshea pays tribute.
726	Shalmaneser V	Hoshea rebels. Siege of Samaria.
722/1	Sargon II	takes Samaria and deports population of Israel.
705	Sennacherib	Revolt of Hezekiah and others. Hezekiah pays tribute. Jerusalem delivered.
681	Esarhaddon	takes Memphis in Egypt.
669	Ashurbanipal	Assyria holds undisputed sway until 652—then rebellions.
630	Ashuretililani	
620	Sinshariskun	
612	Ashuruballit II	Nineveh falls.

The Kings of Syria

BC

c. 880   Benhadad I

c. 840   Hazael

c. 800   Benhadad II

c. 740   Rezin

Glossary

Adoram was sent by Rehoboam to collect the taxes after the meeting of the tribes at Shechem. He was stoned to death.

Ahijah: This prophet tore his new cloak into twelve pieces, giving ten pieces to Jeroboam as a sign that ten of the tribes would follow him. The prophecy was fulfilled at Shechem when the northern tribes refused to serve Rehoboam.

Asherah: This was a wooden pole used in Canaanite worship to represent the goddess. The plural is 'Asherim'.

Baal: The god of the Canaanites. The word means 'lord', and he was regarded as the lord of the land. He gave fertility to the fields and it was only by worshipping him that the farmer could prosper. The chief 'Baal' dwelt on a high mountain in the north but he had local manifestations at different places.

Benhadad: King of Syria. Asa, king of Judah, appealed to him to attack Israel when Baasha, king of Israel, had attacked Judah. Asa persuaded Benhadad to break his treaty with Israel by sending him treasures from the Temple.

Bethel: The word means 'House of God' and it was given that name by Jacob after the dream in which he saw the ladder between earth and heaven. Before that it was known to Abraham as Luz. It was one of the places where Samuel judged Israel. Jeroboam I placed one of his shrines there when the kingdom was divided and a bull image was placed within the shrine. It became a centre of idolatry.

Covenant: This is the word used to describe the relationship between Jahveh and His people. The word means 'solemn agreement' today and it can be thought of in that sense in the Bible. At Mount Sinai Jahveh and Israel pledge themselves to each other. Jahveh promises to be their God and care for them. They promise to obey Him alone. The emphasis in the Bible is, however, that God chose Israel and made a Covenant with them. It was not an agreement between two equals. It was an indication of the grace of God that He was prepared to make it at all.

Day of the Lord: The people of Israel looked forward to a 'Day of the Lord'. This was to be a day when God would intervene in judgment on Israel's enemies. The enemies would be defeated and Israel would be made supreme. The prophets pointed out that when judgment came it would come upon God's people also. Amos claimed that 'The Day of the Lord would be darkness and not light.' He meant that when God came in judgment it would not be a day of rejoicing for Israel, but a day of sorrow.

Eliakim: An official in charge of Hezekiah's household. He conferred with the Rabshakeh of Sennacherib from the walls of Jerusalem. Isaiah had a great regard for him, probably because he supported Isaiah's policy of 'non-resistance'.

Ezion-Geber: A town on the Gulf of Aqaba. It became important at the time of Solomon as a naval base and as a centre for smelting copper and iron. Jehoshaphat attempted to revive its importance but without success. After the time of Uzziah it came to be known as Elath.

Fertile Crescent: The area stretching from the north of Palestine over into the valleys of the Tigris and Euphrates. It owes its name to the fact that it is a crescent shape and is fertile in contrast to the areas of surrounding desert.

High Places: The Canaanites worshipped Baal on hills in various parts of Palestine. They were regarded as the dwelling places of the god. The word 'high place' came to be associated with idolatry and the worship of Baal. Sometimes the people worshipped Jahveh at these high places and the practices of the Canaanites were used. A king who, in the eyes of the historian, was loyal to Jahveh would destroy the 'high places' altogether. Only Josiah and Hezekiah do this and thus these two kings are the only ones who are really 'good kings'.

Jonadab (or **Jehonadab**): The son of Rechab, the founder of the Rechabites. They believed that Israel should return to the more simple life of the wilderness. To protest against the settled life, they refused to build houses or to till fields or to drink wine. Jonadab supported Jehu in his revolution. Jeremiah used the Rechabites as an example of loyalty.

Maacah: Wife of Rehoboam and mother of Abijah. After the death of Abijah she remained as 'queen mother' but her grandson, Asa, took this position away from her because she had made an Asherah.

Megiddo was an old Canaanite capital. Here Barak fought Sisera and the Canaanites were swept away by the waters of the rising river Kishon (Jud 5 *19–21*). According to *II Kings* 9 *27* Ahaziah died here. Pharaoh Necho, on his way to Carchemish, was attacked by Josiah and killed him at Megiddo.

Micaiah: The one prophet who stood alone when the professional prophets had told Ahab that God would be with him if he went to fight at Ramoth-Gilead. Micaiah told Ahab that not only would the battle be a disaster for Israel, but that he himself would be killed.

Moloch: The national god of the Ammonites.

Monolatry: The belief that although there are many gods only one must be worshipped.

Monotheism: The belief that there is only One God in the Universe.

Nehushtan: Literally 'that brass thing'. This was the word used by Hezekiah when he destroyed the brazen serpent in the Temple. The story of this serpent goes back to the days of Moses (Num 21 *8*). A brass serpent was erected on a pole in the wilderness so that the Israelites who had been bitten by poisonous serpents might look at it. Those who looked in faith were healed. It had been placed in the Temple and the people had begun to use it as an idol. Hezekiah removed it with the other emblems of idolatry.

Pekah: King of Israel. Joined with Rezin, king of Syria, in an attack on Judah because Ahaz, king of Judah, would not join the alliance against Assyria.

Polytheism: The worship of many gods.

Rabshakeh: The general in Sennacherib's army who was sent to demand the surrender of Jerusalem.

Ramah: A town just south of Bethel and about five miles north of Jerusalem. It was fortified by Baasha, king of Israel, when he threatened Asa, king of Judah. Asa appealed to Benhadad, king of Syria, who attacked Baasha. Baasha withdrew from Ramah. Asa dismantled it and built Geba and Mizpah with the materials.

Ramoth-Gilead: An important commercial and strategic town east of the Jordan, on the borders of Israel and Syria. It was amongst the places given up by Omri to Syria in order to 'buy her off' and keep peace. When the territories were returned, Syria refused to let Ramoth-Gilead go. Ahab, king of Israel, asked Jehoshaphat, king of Judah, to help him to try to recapture Ramoth-Gilead from the

Syrians. Ahab was killed there. Later Jehoram of Israel and Ahaziah of Judah fought against Syria to recover the place.

Ras Shamra: The ancient Ugarit, a town on the north coast of Palestine. Among hundreds of tablets found there during excavations were many giving information about the Canaanite religion of the period *c.* 1400 BC.

Rechabites: See under 'Jonadab'.

Rezin: King of Syria. See under 'Pekah'.

Righteous: The prophets maintained that Jahveh was righteous. They meant that He stood for the 'right' as expressed in fair dealings between men. Because Jahveh was righteous it meant that righteousness would be victorious. When the prophets use the phrase 'God's righteousness' they mean that God will win the victory for the right. Because God is like this, men must also do right, i.e. they must be just in their dealings with one another.

Shebnah: A steward of the king's house under Hezekiah. He was associated with Eliakim in the negotiations with the Rabshakeh of Sennacherib. He was not popular with Isaiah, probably because he supported a policy of making an alliance with Egypt.

Shechem: A town in the hill country of Israel. Abraham camped here and Jacob bought a piece of ground near Shechem. Joshua called together the tribes to this place after the conquest of Canaan, and here they accepted the Covenant relationship with Jahveh. Shechem was still a centre of unity. Rehoboam came here to be elected king. When Jeroboam chose Shechem as his capital he chose, therefore, a place sacred in the history of the tribes. Because it was a symbol of unity it would help to unite the Northern tribes into a nation.

Shemaiah: A prophet of whom we know nothing except that he forbade Rehoboam to try to subdue the ten tribes by force after the meeting at Shechem. Later, according to the Chronicler, he declared that the invasion by Shishak, king of Egypt, was a punishment for sin.

Shishak: King of Egypt. He gave asylum to Jeroboam when he fled from Solomon. Later Shishak invaded Palestine and took the treasures of the Temple. His own inscriptions at Karnak show that he attacked as far north as Megiddo.

Sons of Levi: Men of the tribe of Levi who were given the duty of caring for the sanctuary.

Syncretism: The 'mixing' of religions. When the Israelites entered Palestine they came into contact with the religion of the Canaanites. Some of the practices of this religion were adopted into the religion of Israel. Jahveh was worshipped at 'high places' and many of the people were tempted to unite their religion with that of the land in order to get good crops. This 'mixing' is called Syncretism.

Tarshish: Tarshish is believed to refer to Tartessus in Spain. It was regarded as the farthest west a ship could sail. Ships of Tarshish were originally ships trading with the far west. Later the phrase was used to describe large, sea-going ships wherever they traded. Jehoshaphat built such ships but they were wrecked.

Transjordan: refers to the part of Palestine on the east side of the River Jordan.

Valley of Hinnom: This valley was south of the city of Jerusalem. A fertility cult was carried on there involving human sacrifice. Josiah destroyed the shrine and defiled the valley so that the worship of the gods of the land could not be carried on there again.

Zedekiah: i. The last king of Judah before the fall of Jerusalem in 586.

ii. The leader of the four hundred prophets who told Ahab to go to Ramoth-Gilead. He struck Micaiah when he foretold disaster.